That Patchwork Place™

Make A Medallion

by Kathy Cook

Interchangeable components for making medallion quilts

DEDICATION

To my family. They are the center of my life.

ACKNOWLEDGMENTS

Many thanks to:

Mary Jo Shook for making the magnificent Lone Star Medallion quilt. It is hand pieced and hand quilted and is a superb example of her needle skills.

Nina Stehman for providing geometric support.

Kathie Connolly for quilting the Peony pillow.

Carola Blankenbeckler for quilting the Carpenter's Wheel and Maple Leaf pillows.

Georgina Fries for treating my quilt tops with such care.

Richard Fries for marking the quilting on the Blue and Blue wall quilt.

Shirley Thompson for allowing me to reprint her lovely Feathered Heart quilting design.

Muriel McLean for allowing her Baskets and Butterflies scrap quilt to be photographed.

The many Amish ladies who provided such beautiful quilting on several of the tops. Their way of life prevents their names from being mentioned here.

And a very special thanks to Carol Strickland whose word processing and moral support have helped to make this book a reality.

Credits:
Photography . . . . Carl Murray
Illustration and Graphics . . . . Stephanie Benson

All quilts made by the author unless otherwise indicated.

Make A Medallion©
©Kathy Cook, 1985

Library of Congress Card Number 85-052033

0-943574-35-8

There can be no doubt about it, medallion quilts are special. Starting with a bold central design to catch the eye and then adding border after border to enhance that center creates a work of art to be treasured for generations to come. Medallions have been revered as the crowning achievements of the accomplished needleworker. Extra time must be allowed for planning, not only the center, but also the basic geometry of the borders and their tricky corners.

These quilts were more often than not the work of one woman. Because there really isn't a point at which the work can be easily divided, the project offered the quilter an opportunity to draw on all her experience and really show off.

When the time came to commemorate a special event, a quilter could take a great deal of pride in knowing she had the ability to memorialize it with a medallion quilt. Many of the presentation quilts we admire in our museums today are the work of loving hands for the preacher or other community celebrity.

The respect these quilts were given and the esteem in which they were held are the reasons we have so many beautiful medallion quilts to admire today. They were given the very best care that a special quilt deserved. Often they were never used at all. We are truly very fortunate to have so many like-new antique quilts to study.

Unfortunately, I have found there can be a negative side to all the esteem heaped on this one beautiful phase of quilt making. When questioning my advanced quilt classes about their desire to tackle a medallion, their response has been, "Oh, no, we are not ready for that yet." It would seem that medallion quilts can be a little intimidating. I hope you will think of this book as a "design-your-own-quilt kit"; all you need supply is the enthusiasm and material. Don't be intimidated. If you are, you'll worry; if you worry you won't have any fun and that's why we started quilting in the first place.

The truth is that a medallion quilt is no harder to make than any other quilt. It just takes a little adjustment in thinking. Instead of planning your quilt in rows of blocks, start thinking of one block as a central figure with a border to enhance that figure.

A nice central block can really sparkle when its colors or shapes are repeated in a bold graphic border. When the two parts work well together they create a new larger design, much more striking than if they had been used separately. It is this feeling of continuity, whether from repeated shapes, colors, or fabrics, that flows through medallions and makes them special. The central design enhancing the border, and the borders re-emphasizing the center, make the total larger than the sum of its parts. Whether you are a beginner or an advanced quilter, the time has come to have some fun and make a medallion quilt.

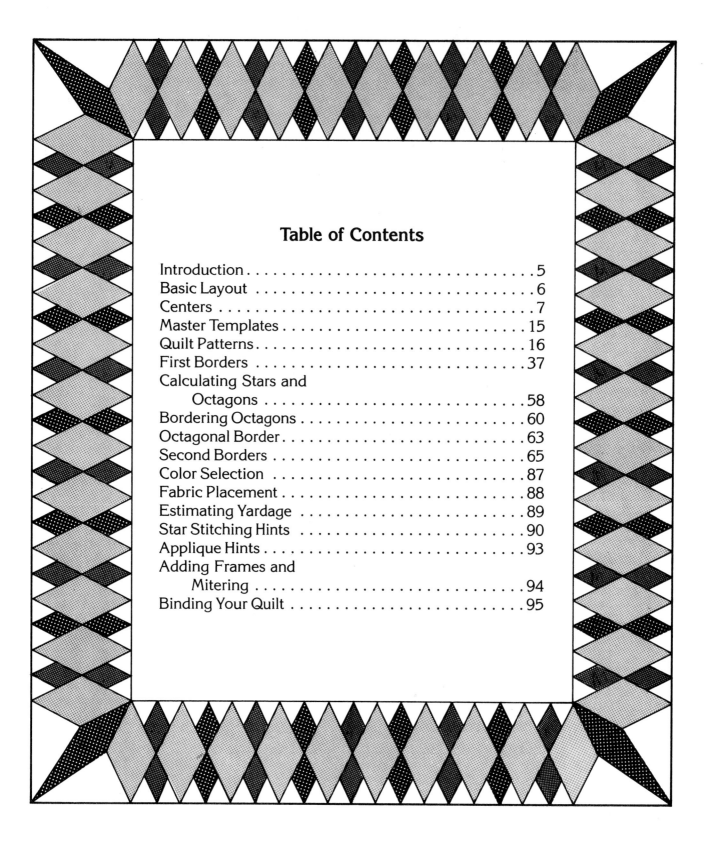

Table of Contents

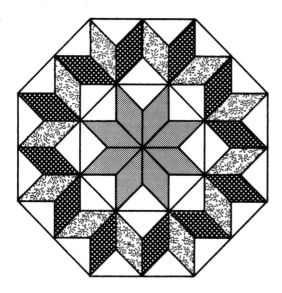

INTRODUCTION

Think of this book as a design workbook. All of the designs have been drafted so that they can be used interchangeably. The line drawings accompanying each pattern have been drawn to the same scale. Tracing paper will be one of your most important design tools. By tracing several of the centers and border patterns you will be able to mix and match them until you have a combination that pleases you. There are over 1,800 combinations so allow extra time to try several.

Once you have a completed tracing of your final design, have it photo copied, and begin experimenting with color. The drawings have purposely been left unshaded so that you will be able to experiment with color, shade, and fabric texture and with their effect on the quilt design. Read the section on color selection and fabric placement if you feel you need direction in this phase of your project.

The master templates (referred to as MT in the instructions) are provided to aid you in designing your own medallion center. All of the center blocks shown are based on the 45° angle of the eight pointed star block. Most are given in their basic form, with large pieces. If you are a beginner you might want to make the block as shown. If you are comfortable working with smaller pieces, try dividing the shapes into smaller units and rearrange them.

There are eight sets of templates. They are based on the 3", 4", 6", 8", 12", 16", 24", and 32" eight-pointed star blocks. There are eleven templates in each set. They include the diamond, square and triangle of the basic star, and eight other shapes made by combining or dividing those three basic shapes. Each template is labeled with the size of the block from which it was derived and a letter designating its shape. As an example — If the directions say "Cut 8 MT-B-16", that means to cut 8 pieces of fabric using Master Template - B (a square) from the 16" block section.

Pay particular attention to the descriptive information about each center pattern. It will give you clues for combining templates from different block sizes to design your own square or octagonal medallion center.

The specific templates for each border are found immediately following their respective pattern. They are labeled "BT", and are numbered in sequence. Remember to transfer all markings to the template pieces as you cut them. A blank grid is provided for both border sizes, should you want to start from scratch and design your own border pattern. By working on tracing paper over the grid you will be assured that your border proportions are the same as those on the basic layout and that the corners turn nicely. The frames can, also, be broken into design units.

At the end of the first border section you will find instructions for calculating the sizes of octagons and octagonal borders. This information will prove invaluable should you want to concentrate on designing with octagons.

A reference section of general quilting information begins on page 87 with suggestions for color selection and fabric placement. It is followed by instructions for estimating yardage, hints for stitching stars and for applique. The balance of the reference section consists of information for finishing your quilt, adding frames and mitering, quilting (there are several quilting patterns given on the large removable sheet in the center of the book) and binding your quilt.

THE BASIC LAYOUT

All the center designs are based on a 32" block. Note, some centers are octagonal. They are still 32" across the width. To separate one design area from another and to provide the inches needed to fit the first borders, 4" frames are necessary. The center square with a 4" frame makes a 40" block; a great size for a newborn-baby quilt or a wall hanging.

By adding one 8" border and another 4" frame, your quilt will become 64" square. This is perfect for napping and is still not too large to be hung most places.

The addition of a second 8" border and 4" frame brings your quilt to an 88" square. This is just right for a double or queen-size coverlet.

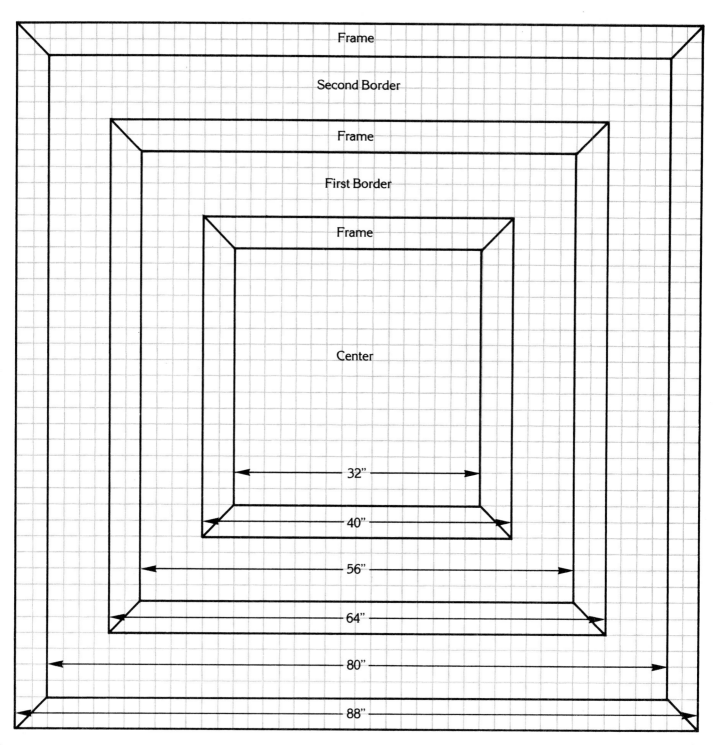

Frame

Second Border

Frame

First Border

Frame

Center

32"

40"

56"

64"

80"

88"

1 square = 2"

CENTERS

There are eighteen center designs shown. All are based on the forty-five-degree angle of an eight-pointed star. They are arranged from the most basic to the most complex. As you progress through the designs, pay particular attention to the descriptive information about each. It will give you a better understanding of the shapes and their relationships to one another. As an exercise, cut colored paper pieces using all of the templates in the 16", 8" and 4" Master Template sections. Play around with them and see what you can come up with. I'm sure you'll be pleased.

THE BASIC STAR

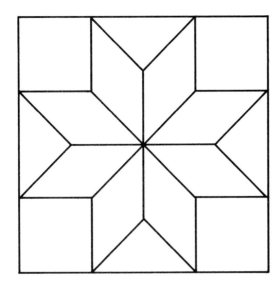

Center pattern #1

The 32" eight-pointed star is the basic block from which all of the center patterns are derived. It can remain square or can be made octagonal by replacing the corner squares with four of the same triangles used on the sides. Even this very simple layout can have many different looks if you alter the fabric placement. Alternating fabrics in the diamonds creates a Le Moyne Star while arranging the fabrics in pairs forms an Arrow of Light.

SPINNING STARS

Both of these striking designs are made by dividing the 32" diamond in half. For the squares and triangles, use the same templates (MT B-32" and MT C-32") used in pattern #1. Use MT F-16" to cut the two pieces needed to reconstruct each diamond. Both of these designs could be made as squares or octagons.

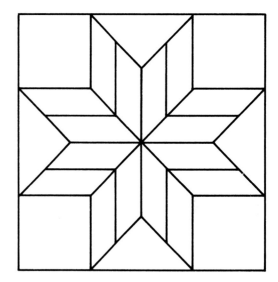

Center pattern #2

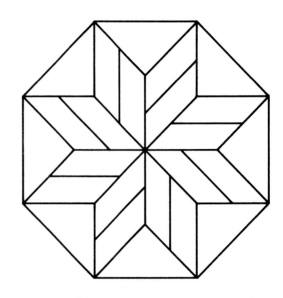

Center pattern #3

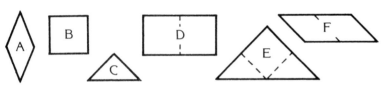

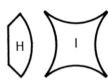

7

SLICED DIAMONDS

These two very simple designs are made by dividing the basic diamond in half. In pattern #4, the diamond has been divided along the center line from each narrow angle. Pattern #5 shows the effect when the diamond is divided along a line connecting the wide angles. Once again use MT B-32" and MT C-32" for the squares and triangles. Use MT J-32" or MT K-32" to reconstruct the necessary diamonds.

Vertically Sliced Diamonds

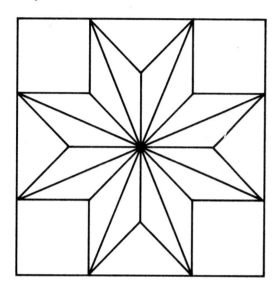

Center pattern #4

Horizontally Sliced Diamonds

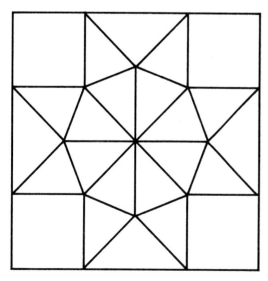

Center pattern #5

VIRGINIA STAR

By dividing the diamond in this 32" square one more time, you have made a Virginia Star. For this pattern you will need to cut four diamonds using MT A-16" for each large diamond.

You can now see a trend developing. Because the length of the side of the smaller diamond is one-half the length of the larger diamond, it is necessary to use the pattern piece from the section of master templates that is one-half the size of the finished square. For example, for a 32" square, use the template from the 16" section.

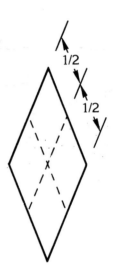

Center pattern #6   Virginia Star

Note that the background pieces have not been divided, so you will still used the square and triangle from the 32" section or just the triangle if you prefer to make this an octagon.

8

LONE STAR

This is the center used for the yellow and turquoise medallion quilt shown on page 20. The side of the basic 32" diamond has been divided four times, so it follows that you would use MT A-8" to reconstruct the large diamonds (32 ÷ 4 = 8).

Once again the background squares and triangles have not been divided so you will still use MT B-32" and MT C-32" for those pieces.

Center pattern #7   Lone Star

STAR AND CUBES

In this pattern the diamonds have remained the same basic shape as used in pattern #1, but the squares and triangles have been divided in half. This division forms a secondary pattern around the central star. Use MT-A-32" when cutting the diamonds. Use master templates B, C, and D from the 16" block section to cut the background pieces. Refer to directions for reconstructing shapes on page 91.

Center pattern #8   Star and Cubes

Don't overlook the possibilities of combining diamonds from different template groups.

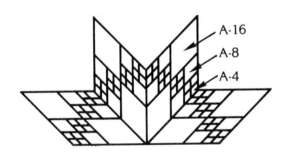

Different template shapes can also be combined to alter the pattern.

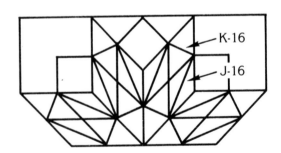

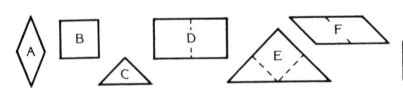

BASIC STAR
WITH BROKEN BACKGROUND

By dividing the background square and triangle one more time, the pattern becomes even more intricate and the design possibilities are greatly increased. Use the template pieces from the section that is one-fourth of the 32" square. (One-fourth of 32"), or MT B-8" and MT C-8".

Remember, it is always possible to combine different multiples of the 8" square and triangle to re-form the large shape. As an example, you could use the 4" or 16" square or triangle to replace some of the 8" pieces in the square. Don't overlook the octagonal possibilities.

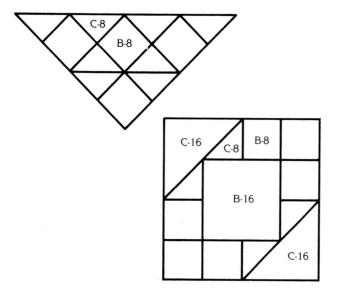

Cut some shapes from colored paper and play around with them.

Center pattern #9

CARPENTER'S WHEEL OR DUTCH ROSE

The traditional Carpenter's Wheel is a lovely old pattern that forms its own medallion by surrounding the central star with a wreath of diamonds. The 32" pattern is developed by rearranging the diamonds, squares, and triangles of a 16" square. This pattern was used for the center of the Christmas Medallion shown on page 77.

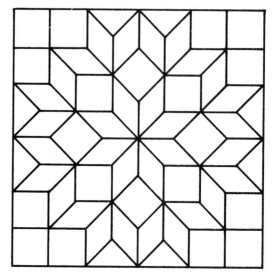

Center pattern #10   Carpenter's Wheel or Dutch Rose

Simply replacing the squares with triangles emphasizes the octagonal shape of this variation.

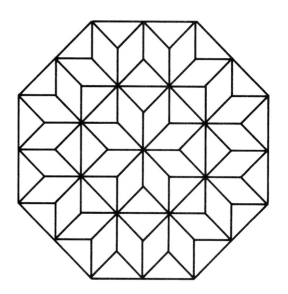

CHRYSANTHEMUM STAR

This 32" chrysanthemum block is made using the same piecing order as the Carpenter's Wheel on page 10. The entire look of it has been changed by replacing the diamond, square, and triangle, from a 16" block with units constructed of shapes cut using 8" master templates. You will need MT A-8", MT B-8", MT C-8", and MT D-8" to make this stunning center design.

Center pattern #11   Chrysanthemum Star

Replace the diamonds, squares and triangles with the following units.

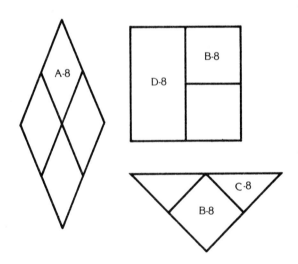

MAPLE LEAF

This charming old pattern goes by many names; my favorite is the Maple Leaf. What a sparkler it would be in fall colors. This 32" block is once again a simple arrangement of the basic shapes of 16" Master Templates.

Center pattern #12   Maple Leaf

By dividing a few of the diamonds in the pattern, the effect is quite different. MT-A-16" has been replaced by MT-J-16".

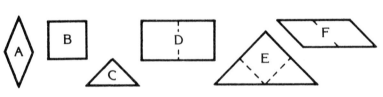

11

BETHLEHEM ROSE

The 32" Bethlehem Rose square is another quick pattern that is adaptable to an octagon. Once again the 16" master templates are used. But this time you will use not only the basic A, B, and C, but E and F as well. The square version of this pattern forms the center of the Bethlehem Rose Medallion on page 79.

Center pattern #13   Bethlehem Rose

For ease in piecing, join the smallest pieces to form larger units that can be stitched in as few straight seams as possible.

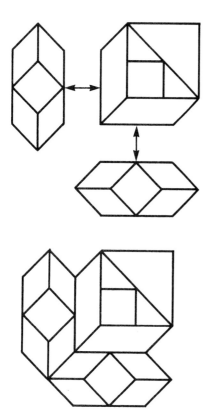

STAR OF THE MAGI

This pattern seems to say, "I want to be an octagon," though it could, of course, be made square. Its name suggests Christmas colors, but tan, red, and navy were chosen to combine with a "preppie stripe". It is shown on page 80. Once again the 16" master templates were used. The pattern could be broken down even farther by using 8" and 4" master templates to reconstruct the basic shapes.

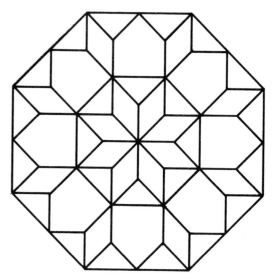

Center pattern #14   Star of the Magi

All star designs will require that you "set in" a few of the pieces. Plan your piecing sequence so that you will be stitching the widest angle possible.

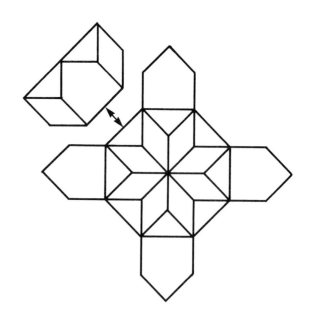

HAND OF FRIENDSHIP

The pattern shown here is just one of the many versions bearing this quaint old name. This one was chosen because its large empty center is so perfect for an applique design. What could be nicer than a presentation quilt personalized with an applique pattern appropriate to the recipient.

The friendship quilt shown on page 18 was made with a friend from Pennsylvania in mind, hence the Lancaster Rose applique and the Philadelphia Pavement border.

Center pattern #15   Hand of Friendship

To avoid having to handle the entire block while adding the last background pieces, complete the 4 corner units before joining them to the center of the block.

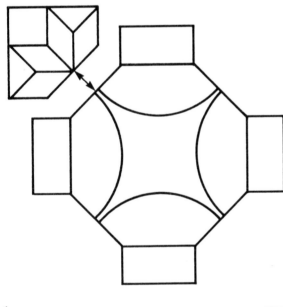

FRIENDSHIP HEART

This Friendship Heart block is the same as the Hand of Friendship with an altered center to allow for an 8" pieced block. The pieces to frame the block should be cut from background fabric. This design was used to make the Welcome Home baby quilt shown on page 17.

Center pattern #16   Friendship Heart

Add Friendship Templates E and F to your favorite 8" block to vary this design.

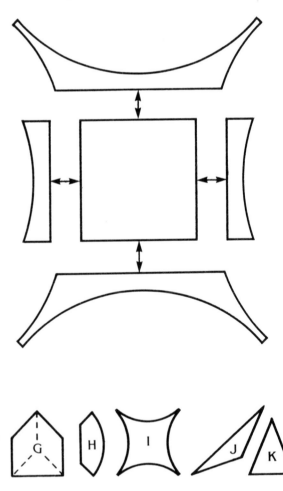

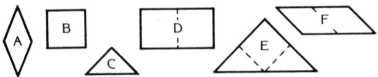

BOUQUET OF PEONIES

All previous patterns have been based on units with the same proportions: 4", 8", 16", and 32". This design illustrates how the 32" block can be divided to combine units from proportionately different groups. The center carnation is a 12" block made with templates from the 12" and 6" block sections. The bouquets of peonies are from the 8" template section. The additional frame strip makes them compatible.

Center pattern #17   Bouquet of Peonies

Use this grid to design your own version of the peony block.

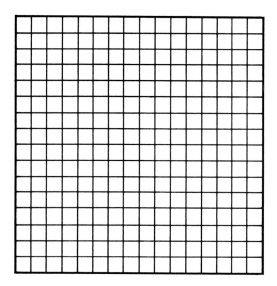

BASKETS AND BUTTERFLIES

The natural combination of baskets and butterflies makes yet another lovely center design. Note how easily a medallion can be made by adding a border around something as simple as an alternating arrangement of two different squares.

In order to accommodate the required 32" center block size, the patterns have been drafted 10 2/3" square. THESE ARE NOT MASTER TEMPLATES AND MUST BE TRACED SEPARATELY.

Center pattern #18   Baskets and Butterflies

This 32" grid is divided into a 9 patch. Each 10 2/3" section is then divided into a small 16-patch. Mix a few of your favorite patterns to create your own center.

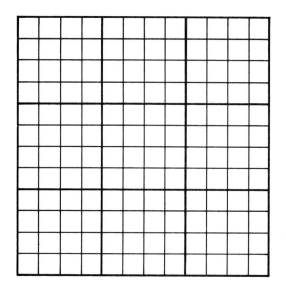

14

MASTER TEMPLATES

The templates on the large folded sheets are used to make the patterns for the center of your medallion quilt. They consist of not only the diamond, square, and triangle, but also of the shapes formed when the three basic shapes are combined in different ways. There are 8 sets labeled: 3", 4", 6", 8", 12", 16", 24", and 32".

They are labeled according to the size block that was drafted to obtain three basic shapes. You could be combining templates from different size groups. It is, therefore, very important that as you cut the templates, you label each with the letter designating its shape and the number designating the measurement of the block from which it was derived.

Each template has been drafted so that you can use them two ways. The dotted line around each is the actual finished size of the piece, no seams allowed. The solid line includes the one-fourth inch seam allowance. Trace the size template that is most appropriate to your stitching methods. Whichever size you choose, remember you must be consistent.

In each section you will find the three basic shapes:
A. Diamond
B. Square
C. Triangle

Additionally, there are combination templates:
D. A rectangle — made by combining 2 squares.

E. A large triangle — made by combining square B and 2 triangles C.

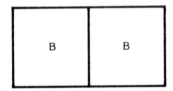

F. A parallelogram — made by combining 2 diamonds A.

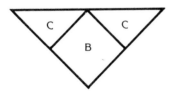

G. A pentagon (5-sided template) made by combining a triangle C with 2 diamonds A.

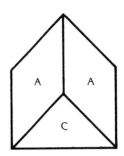

H. and I. These are the 2 additional pieces needed for a Hand of Friendship block. They are labeled according to the size of the finished square.

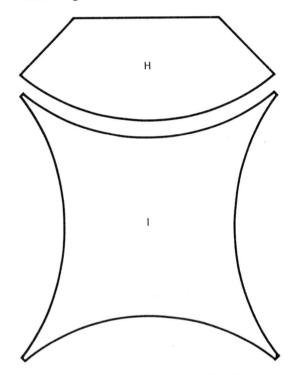

J. A half diamond divided along the line connecting the narrow angles.

K. A half diamond, divided along the line connecting the wide angles.

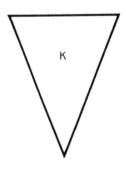

15

QUILT PATTERNS

The following quilts were all designed using center and border patterns from this book. Note how each quilt has its own distinct personality. Even though the proportions of the center and border are the same on every quilt, they appear to be different. The patterns and colors of the fabrics used and the placement of those fabrics contributes to each quilt's individual look.

Pay particular attention to the visual weight of each border design and how it affects the center. Choose your least favorite quilt to determine what characteristics do not appeal to you. We all know what we like and dislike. Being able to determine **why** one design is more appealing than another is a giant step in the decision making process necessary in quilt designing.

RAINBOW STAR BABY QUILT

The basic star center (**#**1) was used to make this charming 40" baby quilt or wall hanging. Eight different solids and one print add interest to this very simple design. Because of the small size required for a newborn baby the strips used in the frame also serve as a border. Dividing the frame into smaller pieces provided an opportunity to repeat all eight solids at the outside edge of the quilt. This adds a sense of unity to the whole quilt.

To make the Rainbow Star Baby Quilt as shown, you will need the following MATERIALS:

    Background print — 2 yards (includes backing)
    8 different solids — 1/2 yd. each
    Batting — 45" x 60"

CUTTING:

    Central block — Use MT A-32", MT B-32", and MT C-32"

From background material —
    Cut 4 MT B-32"
    Cut 4 MT C-32"
    Cut backing 44" x 44"
From each of 8 solids —
    Cut 1 MT A-32"
Borders — Corner squares, use MT A-4", MT B-4", and MT C-4"
From each of yellow, peach, green, and turquoise —
    Cut 8 MT A-4"
    Cut 4 MT B-4"
    Cut 4 MT C-4"
From each of pink, rose, purple, and blue —
    Cut 4 strips 32 1/2" x 1 1/2"
From blue only — Cut 4 binding strips 1 1/2" x 44"

PROCEDURE:

Center:

1.   Lay out diamonds in a color arrangement that pleases you.

2.   Assemble star block following assembly instructions on page 90.

Border:

1.   Join 4 border strips to form each of 4 border units.

2.   Assemble each of 4 corner squares: 1 yellow star with peach background, 1 peach star with yellow background, 1 green star with turquoise background, 1 turquoise star with green background.

3.   Stitch 2 border units to opposite sides of center square.

4.   Stitch 1 corner square to each end of remaining border units.

5.   Stitch completed border units to remaining sides of square.

The vibrant **Rainbow Star Baby Quilt**, 40¨ x 40¨, is the perfect size to welcome a newborn baby. The eight solid colors used for the star center are repeated in the border frame and corner stars, adding a sense of unity to the quilt.

Welcome Home, 40¨ x 40¨, makes an ideal welcome gift for someone special. Vary the 8¨ pieced center block to suit the recipient.

17

Pennsylvania Friendship Quilt, 64" x 64", features a Lancaster Rose applique center and Philadelphia Pavement border. Dusty colors of mauve and green contribute to the delicate antique look.

Basket of Friendship, 64" x 64", is a variation of the Pennsylvania Friendship Quilt featuring a scrap basket center. The chintz look of the polished fabrics gives this quilt a completely different look.

This delicate **Bouquet of Peonies Quilt,** 64" x 64", features thirteen different blue fabrics in the pieced center medallion. Finely detailed quilting in the Prince's Feather pattern fills both the inner and outer frames. The Intertwining Ribbons border, using two shades of pink, contributes to the airy look. A single peony winds through a side border for a touch of contrast.

This exquisite **Lone Star Quilt,** 64" x 64" was pieced and quilted by Mary Jo Shook. The Radiating Star border complements the Lone Star center and adds balance to the overall design. The turquoise and red prints strengthen the quilt while the pale yellow fabric highlights the delicate quilting stitches, especially in the feathered hearts pattern.

LONE STAR QUILT

This exquisite quilt was made by combining the traditional Lone Star center design (#7) and the Radiating Star border design (#1). This particular border was chosen to complement the center design because it had the solid strength necessary to balance the bold center. The turquoise and red prints also add to the strength of the entire quilt. You might choose a different border if paler fabrics are used. The fabric placement was also a consideration, since both the star and the border use the same number of fabrics. Notice how the angles of the pieces in the border direct your eye from the center of the quilt to the corners and back again.

Lone Star Quilt

To make the quilt as shown (64" x 64") on page 20, you will need the following MATERIALS:

Bright yellow print — 1/2 yard
Dark red print — 3/4 yard
Very light turquoise — 1/2 yard
Light turquoise — 1/2 yard
Medium turquoise — 1/2 yard
Dark turquoise — 1/2 yard
Very dark turquoise — 1/2 yard
Light yellow solid — 2 1/2 yards
Backing — 4 yards
Batting — 72" x 96"

CUTTING:

Cutting instructions for the Radiating Star border are on page 38.

Center only — Use MT B-32" and MT C-32", MT A-8"
From bright yellow — Cut 8 MT A-8"
From red print — Cut 32 MT A-8"
From very light turquoise — Cut 16 MT A-8"
From light turquoise — Cut 24 MT A-8"
From medium turquoise — Cut 16 MT A-8"
From dark turquoise — Cut 24 MT A-8"
From very dark turquoise — Cut 8 MT A-8"
From light yellow solid —
    Cut 4 MT B-32"
    Cut 4 MT C-32"
    Cut 4 frame strips 44" x 4 1/2"

PROCEDURE:

1. Arrange 16 small diamonds following the color diagram.

2. Construct large diamond units following instructions for reconstructing shapes on page 91.

3. Assemble units to form a 32" square, following assembly instructions on page 91.

4. Add 4 frame strips and miter corners.

5. Add Radiating Star border found on page 38.

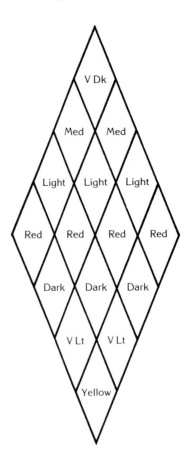

CHRISTMAS MEDALLION

The Carpenter's Wheel center #10 and the Overlapping Diamonds border #2 seem to be a natural combination. It is possible to make either pattern with as few as 3 fabrics. In this case, 4 were used. The large red diamonds in the center appear to be the same size as the diamonds in the border. Beware; they are not cut using the same template.

The red and green plaid strips used for the frame are strong yet do not overpower the other fabrics. They separate the pieced areas yet have a unifying effect on the entire design. Try to visualize this quilt with the frame cut from the background fabric. The border and center might seem to float above the surface of the quilt.

To make the entire quilt as shown (64" x 64"), you will need the following MATERIALS:

Background print — 2 yards
Red print — 1 1/2 yards
Green solid — 2 yards
Green print — 1 3/4 yards
Plaid — 2 1/2 yards
Backing — 4 yards
Batting — 72" x 96"

CUTTING:

Cutting instructions for Overlapping Diamonds border are on page 40.

Center only — Use MT A-16", MT B-16", and MT C-16"
  From background — Cut 16 MT B-16"
     Cut 8 MT C-16"
  From red print — Cut 8 MT A-16"
     Cut 4 MT B-16"
  From green print — Cut 12 MT A-16"
  From green solid — Cut 12 MT A-16"
  From plaid — Cut 4 frame strips 4 1/2" x 44"

PROCEDURE:

1. Join 8 red diamonds to form center star.
2. Set in 8 background squares.
3. Join green diamonds in 8 units as follows:

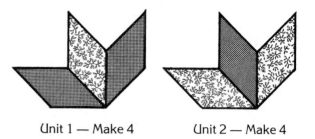

Unit 1 — Make 4   Unit 2 — Make 4

4. Set green units around center, alternating Units 1 and 2.
5. Fill in sides with background triangles.

6. Set in 4 red background squares, following diagram.

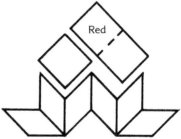

7. Add frame strips and miter corners.
8. Add Overlapping Diamonds border found on page 40.

NOTE: To make this pattern octagonal, eliminate corner square pieces and replace with the same triangles used on the sides.

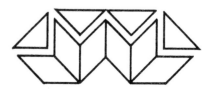

BETHLEHEM ROSE QUILT

Three elements have combined to make this large (88" x 88") quilt: the Bethlehem Rose center (#13), the Swirling Ribbon first border (#3), and the Bethlehem Blossom second border (#3). Study the center pattern for a moment. It is very busy. The stripe, used on the diagonal, moves your eye around the center in a circular motion. Meanwhile, the orange fabric bounces your eye from blossom to blossom. So much activity in one area demands to be balanced by an area of relative calm. The wider angles and large pieces of the first border gently flow around the center and provide that resting place for your eye. The color contributes to the feeling of calm also. Blue has been scientifically proven to be a restful color.

Look now at the last border. Any outer border needs to be tied to the center in some way, either by repeated shapes, fabrics or colors. This border has all three elements. It was designed specifically for this quilt. A portion of the center has been repeated in 8" squares. Look closely at the center and border blossoms. They are not exactly alike but at first glance they appear to be. You could adapt any of the center patterns to use as a border. Be sure to check your original designs on the master grid before you cut your templates.

MATERIALS FOR ENTIRE QUILT:

Light blue dot — 3/4 yard
Dark blue solid — 1 1/2 yards
Medium peach print — 2 yards
Light peach print — 1/2 yard
Rust print — 1 1/4 yards
Stripe - 6 yards
Beige background — 1 yard
Backing — 10 yards
Batting — 90" x 108"

CUTTING:

Cutting instructions for the Swirling Ribbon border are on page 43: Bethlehem Blossom border directions are on page 70.

Center only — Use MT A—16", MT B-16", MT C-16", MT E-16", and MT F-16"
From light blue dot — Cut 8 MT A-16"
From dark blue — Cut 4 MT B-16"
From stripe — Cut 8 MT A-16", reversing template on 4 to match stripe
    Cut 4 frames 42" x 4 1/2"
From medium peach print — Cut 4 MT F-16"
    Cut 4 MT F-16" reversed
From light peach print — Cut 4 MT B-16"
From rust print — Cut 8 MT C-16"

PROCEDURE:

The extra-large pieces in this pattern are easily combined in units to make this block one of the easiest to complete.

Unit 1 — Make 4

Join 2 light blue diamonds and 2 striped diamonds to either side of a dark blue square.

Unit 2 — Make 4

Form a large triangle by joining 2 rust triangles to a light peach square. Join beige triangle E to form a square.

Unit 3 — Make 4

Join 2 medium peach pieces to form a V.

1. Join the 4 #1 units to form a light blue star in the center.

2. Set 1 unit #2 in each unit #3 and join to match main star unit.

3. Fill in sides with remaining triangles C.

4. Add frame strips and miter corners.

5. Add Swirling Ribbon and Bethlehem Blossom borders.

PREPPIE MEDALLION

The Star of the Magi center (#14) is just one of the many center block designs that is adaptable to an octagon. I have combined it with the Basic Border to fit an octagon (page 60). Because this border is made using Master Templates, it is one of the most versatile of all the border designs given. Any 32" center design can be scaled down and repeated in the 16" and 8" sections of the border. The 16" corner sections can be filled with blocks that are made with templates that are one half the size of the ones used to make the 32" center. The 8" blocks along the sides of the quilt can be made with templates that are one-fourth the size of the center design.

By using the same templates to make the navy blue center star and the four corner stars, not only was the fabric repeated in the border, but it was repeated in the same shape pieces in the same size. This balances the center and border so completely that the quilt appears to be one large block design rather than a center and border. The strong graphic look of this quilt might be just what you need to brighten a corner of your home.

MATERIALS to make the Preppie Medallion as shown (64" x 64"):

Dark red print — 1 yard
Navy print — 1 yard
Red solid — 3/4 yard
Tan — 2 yards
Stripe — 2 1/2 yards
Backing — 4 yards
Batting — 72" x 90"

CUTTING: Instructions for the Basic Octagon border are shown on page 60.
Center only — Use MT A-16", MT C-16", and MT G-16"
    From navy print — Cut 16 MT A-16"

From dark red print — cut 4 MT G-16".
From red solid — Cut 4 MT G-16"
From tan — Cut 24 MT C-16"
From stripe — Cut 8 frame strips 20" x 4 1/2", matching stripe on each
Cut 4 binding strips 1 1/2" x 72"

PROCEDURE:

1. Join 8 navy print diamonds to form center star.
2. Set in 8 tan triangles to form octagon.
3. Join 4 red solid pentagons (G) to center.

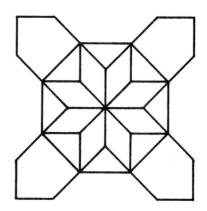

4. Construct units by joining 1 navy print diamond to each side of 4 red print pentagons.
5. Set in 2 triangles to each unit.

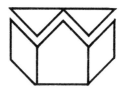

6. Insert units between red solid pentagons (G) around center.

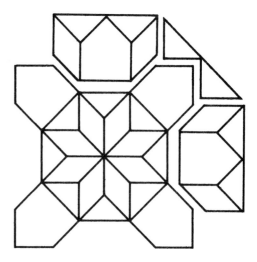

7. Add remaining 8 tan triangles to complete octagon.
8. Add frame strips and miter corners. See mitering instructions on page 94.
9. Add Basic Octagonal border found on page 60.

24

PENNSYLVANIA FRIENDSHIP QUILT

This charming quilt was made with a specific theme in mind. Because it was to be for a friend from Pennsylvania, patterns relating to that area were chosen and adapted to coordinate. The large open area of the Hand of Friendship center (#15) was an ideal place for personalized applique. The Philadelphia Pavement border (#5) was not only appropriate to the theme but it required only the three fabrics used in the center.

Because the border is solidly colored, the strips for the frame were made from the background fabric. They serve to divide the design areas rather than become part of them. Try to imagine the same quilt with the frame made from a fourth print. The frame would blend with the border and make it look 16" wide, much too strong for the open center with its delicate applique.

To make the quilt as shown (64" x 64"), you will need the following MATERIALS:

Background print — 2 3/4 yards
Light rose — 3/4 yard
Dark rose — 1 1/4 yards
Green — 1 yard
Backing — 4 yards
Batting — 72" x 90"

CUTTING: Instructions for the Philadelphia Pavement border are on page 50.
Center only — Use MT A-16", MT B-16", MT C-16", MT D-16", MT H-32" and MT I-32".
Tan background print —
Cut 4 MT B-16"
Cut 8 MT C-16"
Cut 4 MT D-16"
Cut 1 MT I-32"*
Cut 4 frame strips 44" x 4 1/2"

From green —
Cut 4 MT H-32"
Cut 4 large leaves for applique
Cut 8 small leaves for applique
From light rose —
Cut 8 MT A-16"
Cut 4 small hearts for applique
Cut 1 small circle for applique
From dark rose —
Cut 8 MT A-16"
Cut 4 large hearts for applique
Cut 1 large circle for applique

* To avoid unduly stretching the narrow points of piece I while appliqueing, cut a large square around drawn pattern. Trim to desired shape after completing applique.

PROCEDURE:

1. Applique Lancaster Rose on center of piece I. Refer to applique hints on page 93. Follow placement diagram on page 26.

2. Join 4 curved H pieces around I. Trim excess seam allowance.

3. Join 4 rectangular pieces D.

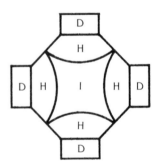

4. Construct 4 corner units by joining 4 diamonds and setting in 2 triangles and 1 square.

5. Set in corner units.

6. Add 4 frame strips and miter corners.

7. Add Philadelphia Pavement border found on page 50.

Applique Placement and Templates
Hand of Friendship Center

Templates:
Carefully trace the Heart and Leaf templates onto graph or tracing paper. Add 1/4" seam allowance on all sides before cutting fabric.

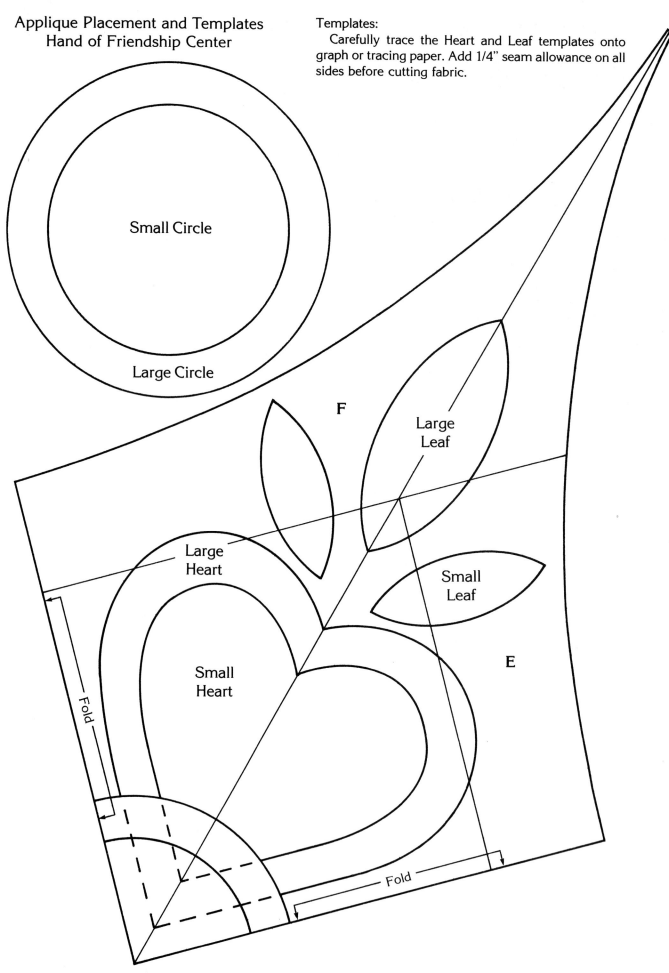

Small Circle

Large Circle

F

Large Leaf

Small Leaf

Large Heart

Small Heart

E

Fold

Fold

WELCOME HOME

What nicer way is there to welcome someone than with this darling quilt. By using the Friendship Heart Center (#16) and treating the frame strips as borders you have a beautiful 40" x 40" wall hanging or nap quilt.

Any eight inch block pattern could be substituted for the heart. You might want to use one that has particular meaning to a friend and then combine it with a border named for their occupation or locale. If you used the Album Border (second border #2) it would make a wonderful presentation quilt.

The pattern for an 8" pieced heart is included for fun. What a pretty baby quilt it would make with the name embroidered in the heart.

To make the baby quilt as shown on page 17, you will need the following MATERIALS:

Light background — 3/4 yard
Flower print — 1/2 yard
Light blue print — 3/8 yard
Light pink print — 1/4 yard
Dark blue print — 5/8 yard
Backing — 1 3/8 yards
Batting — 45" x 60"

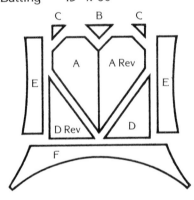

CUTTING: For heart center, use Heart Templates A-F.

From flower print —
    Cut 1 A
    Cut 1 A reversed
From background —
    Cut 1 B
    Cut 2 C
    Cut 1 D
    Cut 1 D reversed
    Cut 2 E
    Cut 2 F

For remainder of quilt, use MT A-16", MT B-16", MT C-16", MT D-16", and MT H-32".

From flower print —
    Cut 8 MT A-16"
    Cut 4 strips 2 1/2" x 45"
From background —
    Cut 4 MT B-16"
    Cut 8 MT C-16"
    Cut 4 MT D-16"
From light pink —
    Cut 8 MT A-16"
From dark blue —
    Cut 8 strips 1 1/2" x 45"
    Cut 4 strips 1 1/2" x 45" for binding
From light blue —
    Cut 4 MT H-32"

PROCEDURE:

1. Join 2 As to form heart.
2. Set in B.
3. Join Cs and Ds to complete square.
4. Join Es to opposite sides of square.
5. Join Fs to complete center.
6. Complete 32" square following directions for Hand of Friendship center #13.
7. Construct each border strip by joining 1 dark blue strip to each long edge of flowered strip.
8. Join borders to quilt center and miter corners.

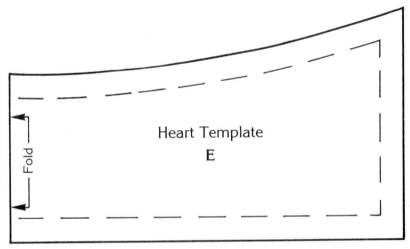

Heart Template
E

Fold

27

Heart Templates

Heart Template
B

Heart Template
D

Heart Template
A

Fold

Heart Template
F

Heart
Template
C

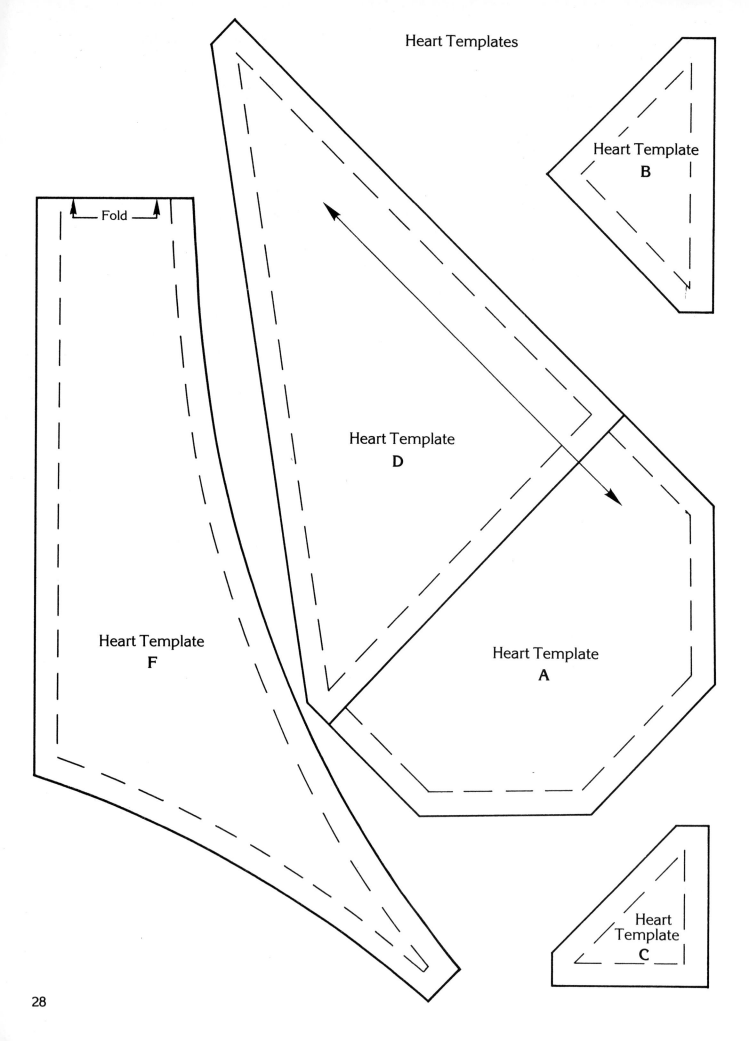

BOUQUET OF PEONIES

The Bouquet of Peonies center (#17) has that airy look that seems to require a light weight border. The Intertwining Ribbons border (#4) was the logical choice. The colors used in this delicate quilt contribute to its feminine look. This quilt would be equally attractive in Christmas colors. By appliqueing small yellow circles to the centers of red "peonies", you could change them to poinsettias.

The "peonies" could be changed to chrysanthemums if half size templates were used to reconstruct each flower. Shades of yellow and gold would certainly carry out the theme, particularly if the dark green stems were tied with copper colored ribbons.

To make the quilt as shown (64" x 64") on page 19, you will need the following MATERIALS:
Light pink — 3/4 yard
Dark pink — 3/4 yard
White — 4 1/2 yards
Blue, pink and white print for carnation and
    border star — 1/4 yard
12 different blue and white prints — 1/8 yard each
Green solid — 1/2 yard
Green print — 1/2 yard
Backing — 4 yards
Batting — 72" x 90"

CUTTING: Instructions for the Intertwining Ribbons border are on page 46.

To make the 32" square you will need MT A-12", MT B-6", MT C-6", MT D-6" and MT A-8", MT B-8" and MT C-8", plus an additional frame piece and the applique shapes provided here.
From light pink —
    Cut 4 applique pieces A
    Cut 4 applique pieces A reversed
    Cut 4 applique pieces C

From dark pink —
    Cut 4 applique pieces B
    Cut 4 applique pieces B reversed
    Cut 4 applique pieces D
    Cut 4 applique pieces D reversed
From white —
    Cut 4 carnation frames
    Cut 4 MT B-6"
    Cut 8 MT C-6"
    Cut 4 MT D-6"
    Cut 48 MT B-8"
    Cut 48 MT C-8"
    Cut 4 frame strips 44" x 4 1/2"
From green print —
    Cut 8 MT B-6"
    Cut 24 MT A-8"
From green solid —
    Cut 3 yards bias strips, 1" wide
From each of 12 blue and white prints —
    Cut 6 MT A-8"
From blue, pink and white print —
    Cut 8 MT A-12"

PROCEDURE:
Center carnation — 12" block with 2" frame.
1. Construct 4 corner units following diagram.
2. Construct 4 triangle units following diagram.

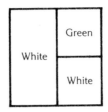 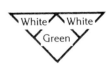

3. Assemble 12" star block following assembly instructions on page 90.
4. Set in square and triangle units to complete block.

5. Join carnation frames and miter corners.

Peony blocks — 8" square

Each of the twelve blocks is made from a different blue print fabric. Using the same green "leaf" fabric with all of the peonies provides a sense of continuity.

1. Assemble twelve 8" star blocks. Make sure to set in a square between the 2 green leaves to position them properly in the larger square.

Assembling the 32" square

1. Make 2 short side strips by joining 2 peony squares. Check leaf placement with diagram. Stitch to opposite sides of carnation squares.

2. Make 2 long side strips by joining 4 peony squares. Stitch to remaining sides of center.

3. Complete applique following directions below.

4. Add frame strips and miter corners.

5. Add Intertwining Ribbons border found on page 46.

APPLIQUE:

The very small amount of applique on this cheery quilt adds another dimension to it altogether. The gentle curves of the bows and stems, in contrast with the sharp angles of the diamonds, form soft resting places for the eye as it moves around the quilt. Read over the section of applique hints found on page 93 before you begin.

1. Position short stem pieces following placement diagram and baste to background. Remove a few stitches in leaf corners and tuck stem ends under leaves. Close seam while appliqueing stem to background.

2. Baste long stem piece in place, covering raw ends of short pieces. Applique.

3. Position and applique bow pieces in the following order: Streamers, Side pieces, Center.

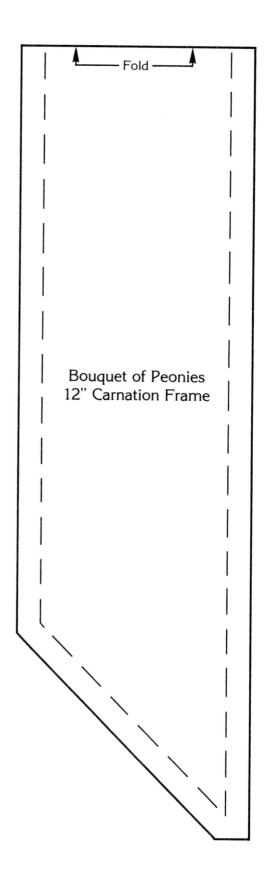

Bouquet of Peonies
12" Carnation Frame

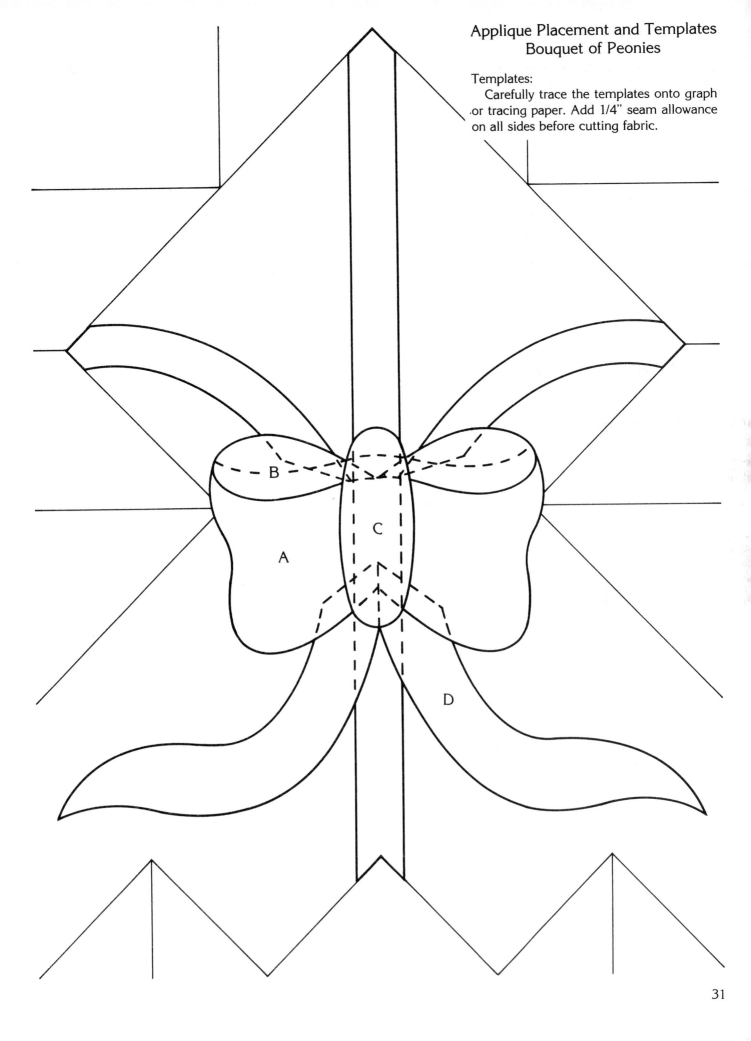

Applique Placement and Templates
Bouquet of Peonies

Templates:
   Carefully trace the templates onto graph or tracing paper. Add 1/4" seam allowance on all sides before cutting fabric.

B

A

C

D

BASKETS AND BUTTERFLIES

In combining the Baskets and Butterflies center (#18) with the Dresden Blossom border (#6), several factors were considered. Both the border and the center have many pieces and were easily adaptable to using eight different solid fabrics. Both represent objects rather than being purely geometric. And, most importantly, the gentle curves of the border provide nice contrast to the sharp angles of the center design. Notice the butterflies scattered throughout the quilting. Repeating a theme or motif will always add a sense of unity to any design.

To make the entire quilt as shown on page 78, you will need the following MATERIALS:
Purple solid — 5 yards
Light green print — 1 1/2 yards
8 different pink and lavender solids — 1/2 yd. each
Backing — 4 yards
Batting — 72" x 90"
CUTTING: Directions for Dresden Blossom border are on page 52.
Center square only —
Baskets — Make 5
From dark purple —
Cut 10 B
Cut 10 C
Cut 5 D
Cut 5 E
Cut 5 E reversed*
From light green —
Cut 5 F
Cut 10 G

* These pieces are easily stitched incorrectly. Make a dot in the seam allowance in the outside corner to avoid confusion.

From 8 assorted solids —
Cut 20 A

Butterflies — Make 4
From dark purple —
Cut 4 A
Cut 4 A reversed
Cut 4 B
Cut 4 B reversed
Cut 8 C
Cut 16 H frames
From assorted solids —
Cut 4 D
Cut 4 D reversed
Cut 4 E
Cut 4 E reversed
Cut 4 F
Cut 4 F reversed
From light green —
Cut 8 G

PROCEDURE FOR BASKETS:

1. Join diamonds to form 1/2 star.
2. Set in 2 corner squares and 1 triangle.
3. Add 2 pieces B to complete top half of block.

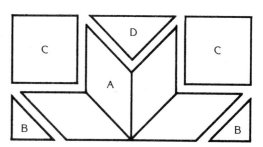

4. Join pieces E and G to form large triangle unit.

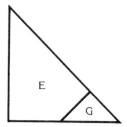

5. Stitch 1 triangle unit to each side of piece F to form bottom half of block.

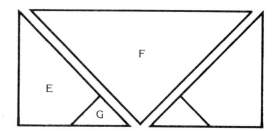

6.   Join 2 halves to complete square.

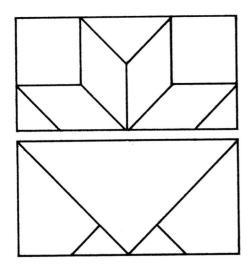

PROCEDURE FOR BUTTERFLIES:

The 8 pieces of the butterfly come together in the center just like a star. Piece them easily by applying the same methods used for star blocks.

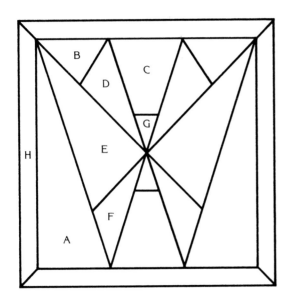

1.   Join B and D following diagram. Treat as 1 piece (BD), reversing for BD Reversed.

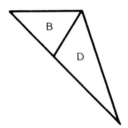

2.   Join pieces E and F. Treat as 1 piece (EF).

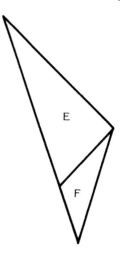

3.   Join pieces C and G. Treat as 1 piece (CG).

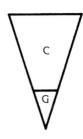

4.   Join BD to EF. Add CG.
5.   Join halves of butterfly.
6.   Add 1 piece A to each side.

7.   Add 4 frame strips to complete 10 2/3" block.
8.   Join the 9 completed squares in 3 rows of 3 blocks each. Add 4 frame strips and miter the corners.
9.   Add Dresden Blossom border found on page 52.

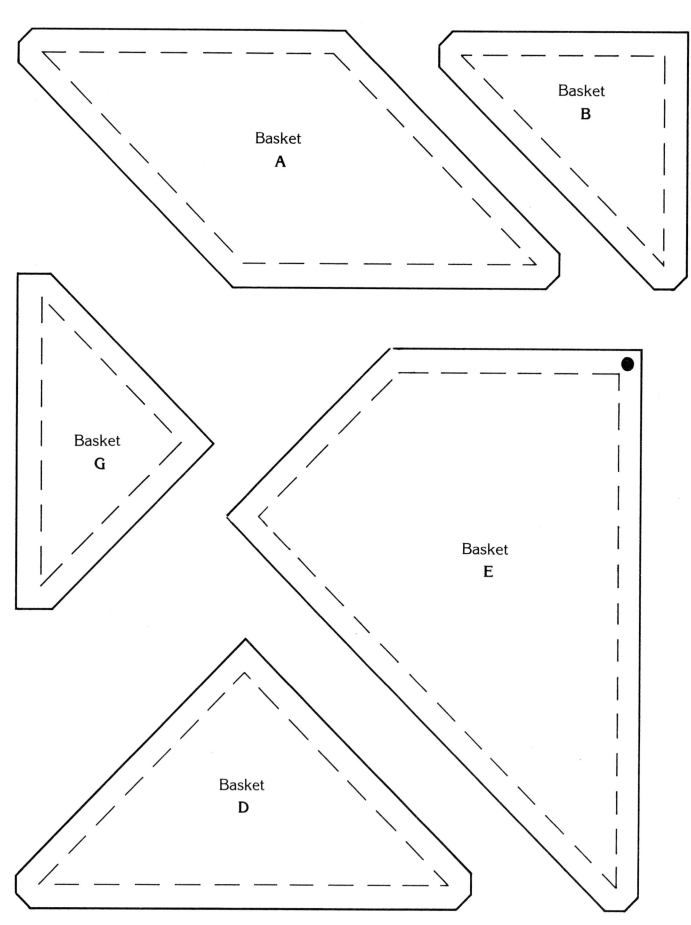

Basket
A

Basket
B

Basket
G

Basket
E

Basket
D

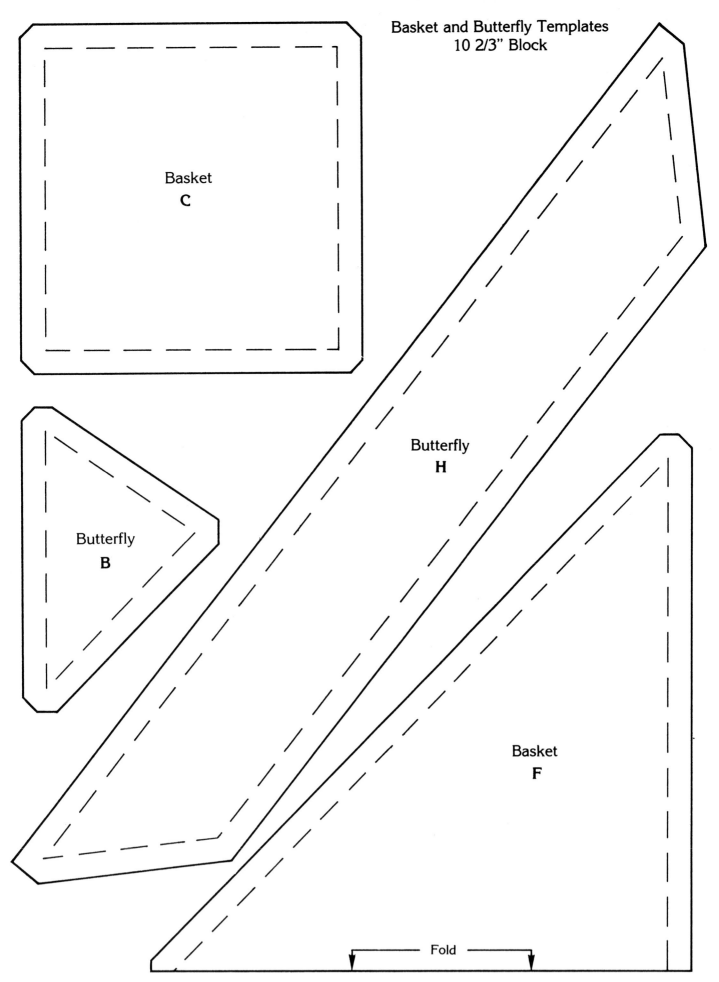

Basket and Butterfly Templates
10 2/3" Block

Basket
C

Butterfly
H

Butterfly
B

Basket
F

Fold

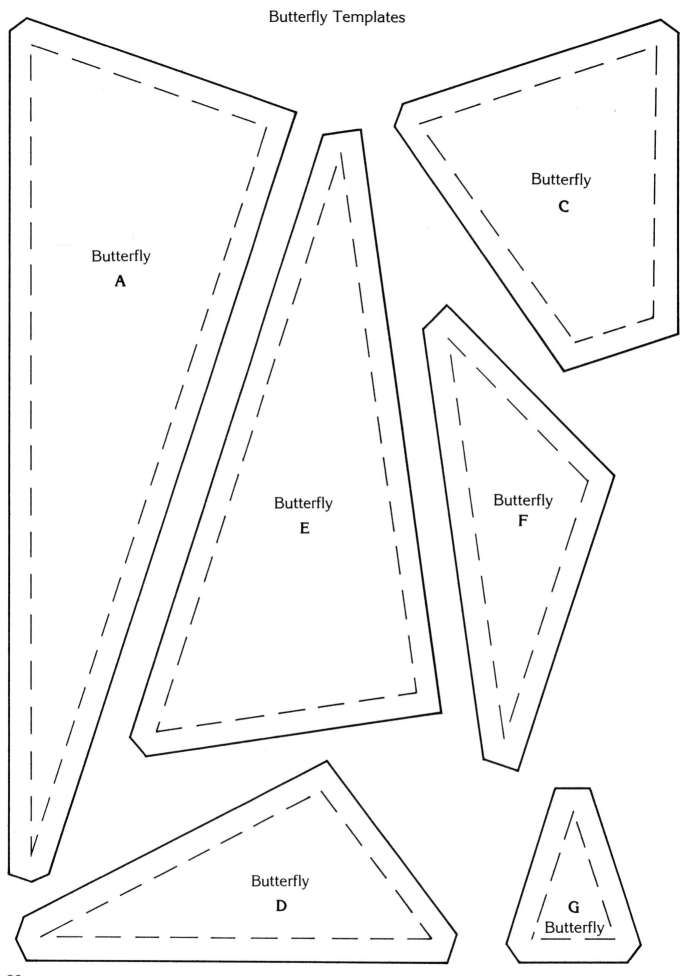

Butterfly
A

Butterfly
C

Butterfly
E

Butterfly
F

Butterfly
D

G
Butterfly

FIRST BORDERS

CHOOSING A BORDER:

There are several things to consider when you decide on a border. The shape of the pieces should be the first consideration. Lay your traced center pattern (including frames) over several borders. This will give you a picture of how the border shapes blend with the center design. Does it please you? It isn't necessary to have studied design to know what you like. Some of the combinations will look as though they belong together. Others can be eliminated right away.

Once you have decided on two or three possible border designs, take the time to color them in. I have purposely left the designs unshaded so that you would not be influenced by my thoughts about color placement. Make tracings of your completed designs using several different borders. Make photocopies of each and spend some time coloring each differently. You now have a very clear picture of what your quilt will look like, not only in your mind, but also on paper.

Because the color selection has been left to you, you will be estimating the yardage amounts. Take the time to count the number of shapes in each color and write it down. This will make the estimating process less complicated.

Many of the borders are made using master templates in combination with new shapes labeled border templates, (referred to as BT in cutting directions). Clearly label each template as you cut it to avoid confusion.

NOTE: Many of the borders in the First Borders section are based on units that are 4" or 8" wide. Some of these designs can be used as second borders by adding extra units. Try to trace them with extra units and lay the tracing over the master grid in the Second Borders section. If the center units can be adjusted and the corners still fit nicely, you can use them. Remember, if it works on the drawing it will work in the quilt.

MASTER GRID
FIRST BORDERS

Use this master grid to plan your own first border for your quilt. Remember, one square on the grid equals two square inches on the quilt. Draft the templates their actual size using graph paper.

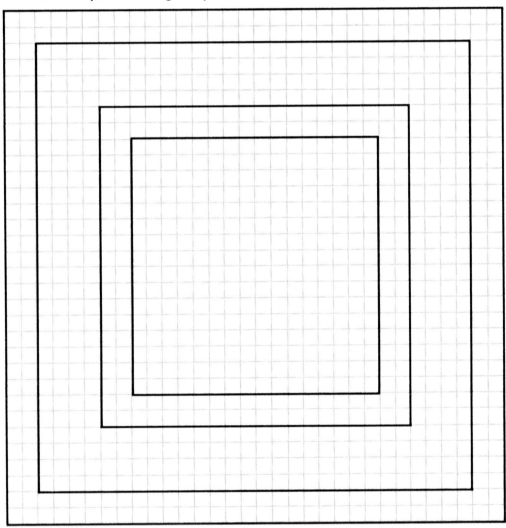

RADIATING STAR

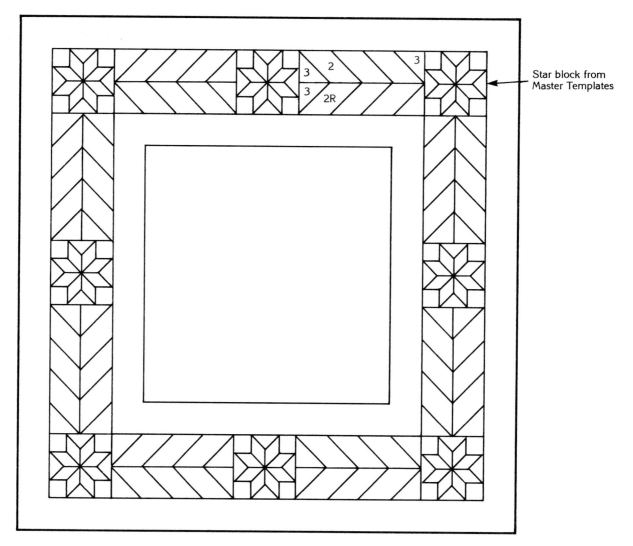

Star block from Master Templates

First Border #1

Radiating Star

This is the border design that was used to complete the Lone Star Medallion on page 20. The large pieces form a solid band of color around the center square. The angle of the parallelograms repeats the angles of the stars and gives them a radiating effect.

If you have chosen to color your border as shown in the Lone Star Medallion you will need to cut the following:

CUTTING:
Use MT A-8", MT B-8", and MT C-8" for star blocks
Use BT #2 and BT #3 for border strips
From bright yellow print —
    Cut 32 MT A-8"
From dark red print —
    Cut 32 MT A-8"

From very light turquoise —
    Cut 16 MT B-8"
    Cut 16 MT C-8"
    Cut 16 BT #3
From light turquoise —
    Cut 8 BT #2
    Cut 8 BT #2 reversed
From medium turquoise —
    Cut 8 BT #2
    Cut 8 BT #2 reversed
From dark turquoise —
    Cut 8 BT #2
    Cut 8 BT #2 reversed
From very dark turquoise —
    Cut 16 BT #3
    Cut 16 MT B-8"
    Cut 16 MT C-8"
From light yellow solid —
    Cut 4 frame strips 68" x 4 1/2"
    Cut 4 binding strips 72" x 1 1/2"

PROCEDURE:

1. Make 4 red stars with very light turquoise background. Make 4 yellow stars with very dark turquoise background. Follow assembly instructions on page 91.

2. Join border pieces in rows following diagram.

3. Join rows to complete unit.

4. Make 4 border strips by stitching 1 border unit to each side of a red star block.

5. Join 2 border strips to opposite sides of center.

6. Stitch 1 yellow star block to each end of remaining border strips.

7. Join to remaining sides of center.

8. Add 4 frame strips and miter corners.

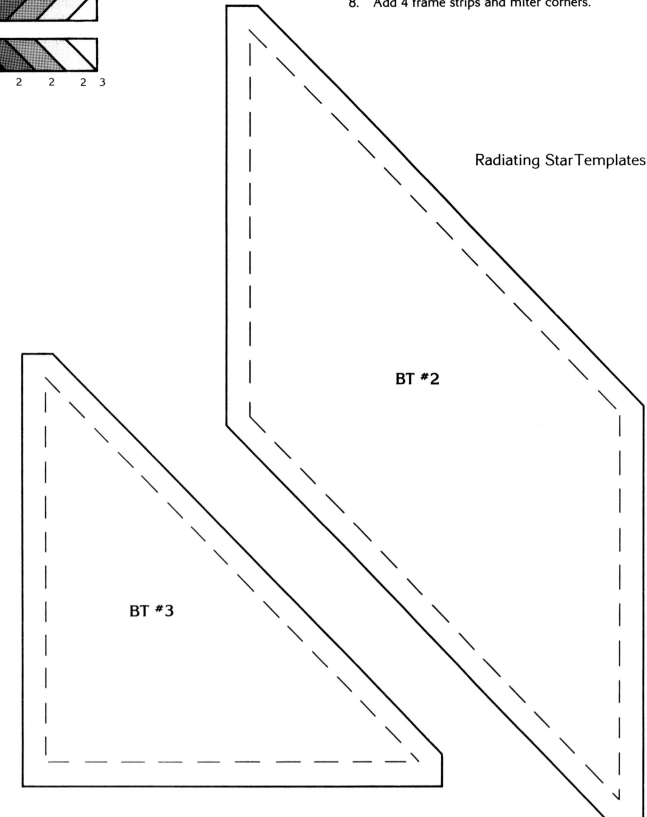

3   2   2   2   3

Radiating Star Templates

BT #2

BT #3

OVERLAPPING DIAMONDS

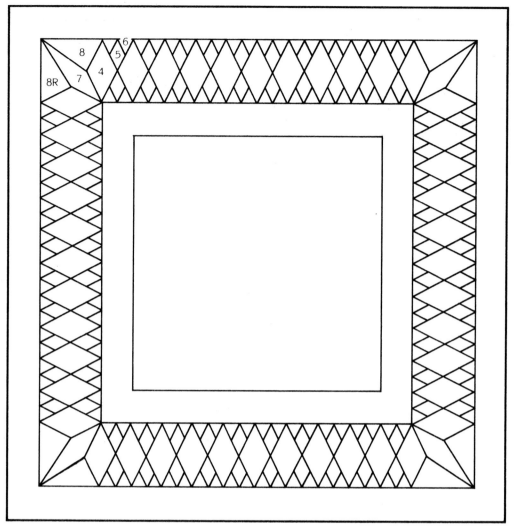

First Border #2

Overlapping Diamonds

This bright border has more than the average number of pieces, but I'm sure you will agree that it is well worth the extra effort. It was used to make the Christmas Medallion on page 77. The shapes appear to be the same ones used to make the Carpenter's Wheel block, but they are NOT and must be cut separately.

To color the border as I have in the Christmas Medallion you will need to cut the following:

Use BT #4, BT #5, BT #6, BT #7, and BT #8
From background print —
    Cut 160 BT #6
    Cut 4 BT #8
    Cut 4 BT #8 reversed

From red print —
    Cut 44 BT #4
From green solid —
    Cut 40 BT #5
    Cut 2 BT #7
    Cut 4 binding strips 72" x 1 1/2"
From green print —
    Cut 40 BT #5
    Cut 2 BT #7
From plaid — Cut 4 frame strips 68" x 4 1/2"

PROCEDURE:

1. Join 2 background triangles to 2 sides of each green diamond to form triangle units.

2. Join 1 print triangle unit and 1 solid triangle unit to opposite sides of 36 diamonds to make 36 diamond units.

3. Construct each of 4 border strips by joining 9 diamond units. Reverse shapes when stitching to match solid to solid and print to print of small diamonds.

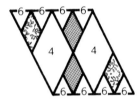

4. Add 1 print and 1 solid triangle unit to each end to fill in border strip.

5. Construct 2 corner units as follows:
   a. Join 2 red diamonds to BT #7 cut from print.
   b. Set in 2 BT #8 to complete the corner.

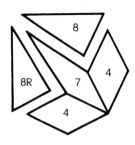

6. Construct remaining 2 corner units using BT #7 cut from solid.

7. Stitch border strips to each side of center.

8. Set in corner units, alternating prints and solids.

9. Join 4 frame strips and miter corners.

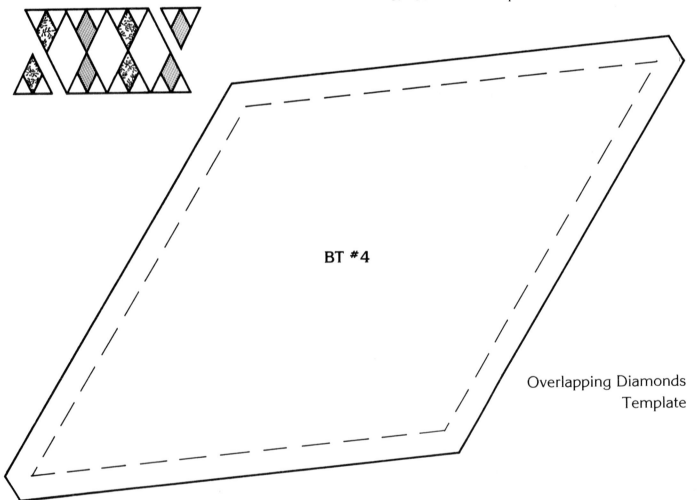

BT #4

Overlapping Diamonds
Template

41

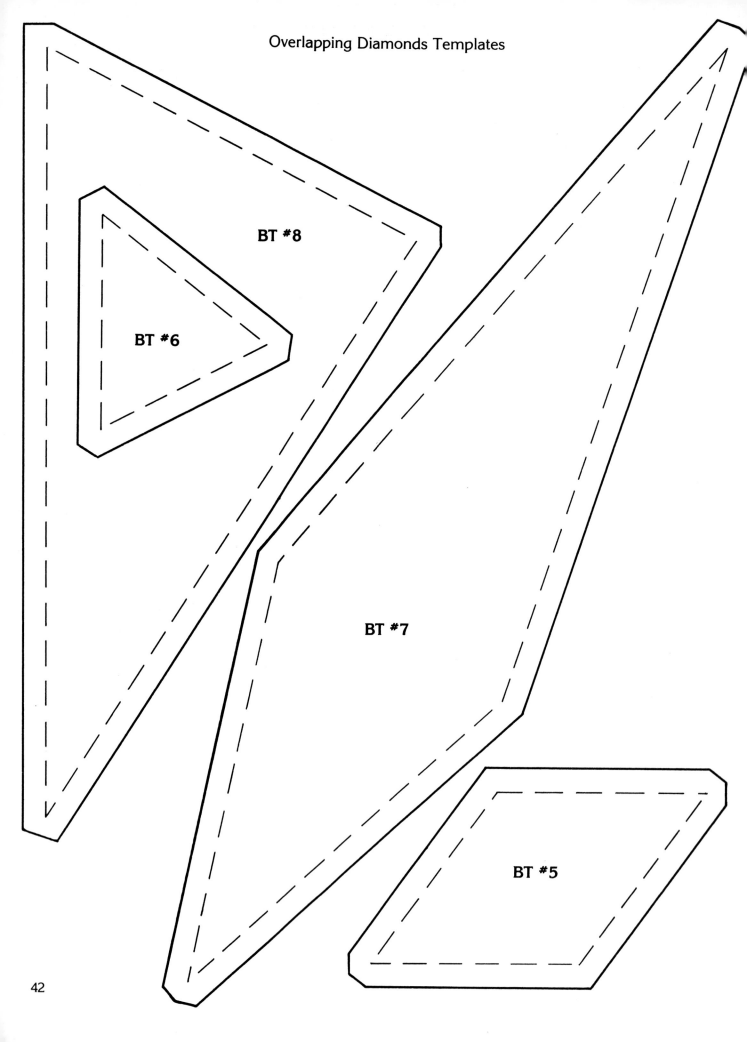

Overlapping Diamonds Templates

BT #8

BT #6

BT #7

BT #5

SWIRLING RIBBON

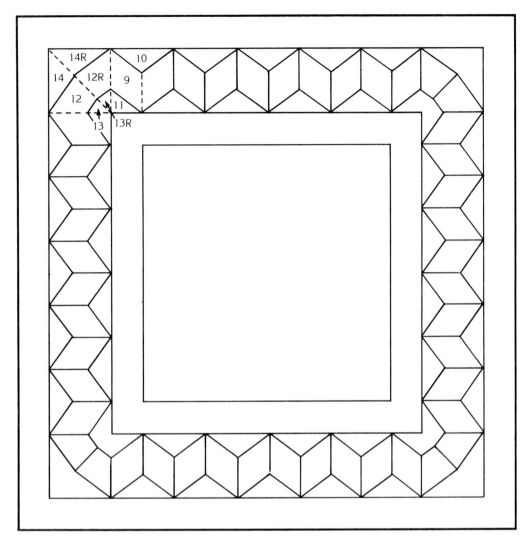

First Border #3   Swirling Ribbon

All designs have a focal point, the point on the quilt where the eye begins to travel. If the center is "busy" and forces your eye to jump from place to place, this Swirling Ribbon border can add the contrast you need. Its large pieces with gentle angles form a border that seems to flow calmly around the center.

To color this border as I have in the Bethlehem Rose Medallion on page 79, you will have to cut the following:

Use BT #9, BTG#10, BT #11, BT #12, BT #13, and BT #14
From light blue dot —
    Cut 16 BT #9

From dark blue solid —
    Cut 36 BT #10
    Cut 4 BT #11
    Cut 4 BT #11 reversed
    Cut 4 BT #13
    Cut 4 BT #13 reversed
    Cut 4 BT #14
    Cut 4 BT #14 reversed
From stripe —
    Cut 12 BT #9
    Cut 12 BT #9 reversed
    Cut 4 BT #12
    Cut 4 BT #12 reversed
    Cut 4 frame strips 68" x 4 1/2"
Remember to match stripe when cutting reverse pieces.

PROCEDURE:

In this type of border, I find it easier to start at one end of the border strip and build to the other. Remember: do not stitch past seam lines.

Make 4 border strips

1. Stitch 1 BT #11 to 1 side of striped BT #9.

2. Continue building the border strip in this manner, following the diagram.

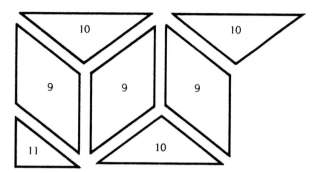

3. Join BT #10 to opposite side of BT #9.

4. Set in light blue BT #9.

5. Join another BT #10 to fill in strip.

6. Set in another striped BT #9.

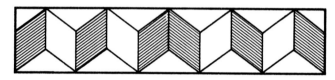

7. Construct each of 4 corner squares as follows:

    a. Make triangles by joining blue pieces BT #13 and BT #14 to piece BT #12.

    b. Make a mirror image triangle by joining pieces BT #13 reversed and BT #14 reversed to piece BT #12 reversed.

    c. Stitch 2 triangles together matching stripes.

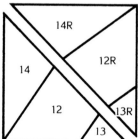

8. Join 2 border strips to opposite sides of center.

9. Stitch corner square to each end of remaining border strips, matching stripes.

10. Join long strips to remaining sides of center.

11. Add frame strips and miter corners.

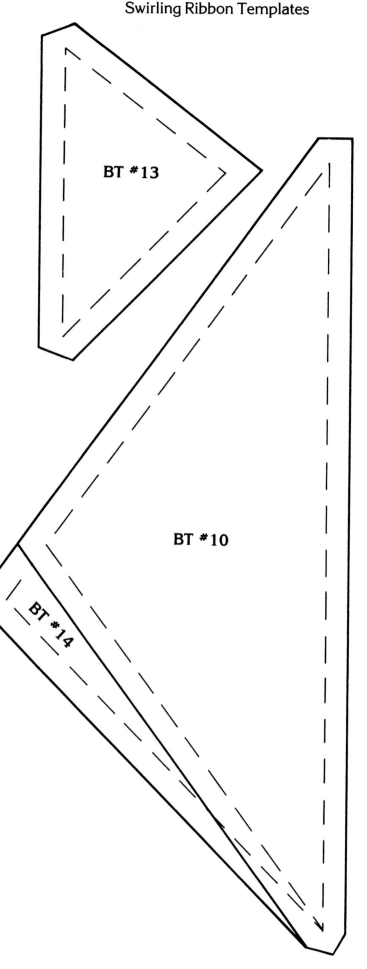

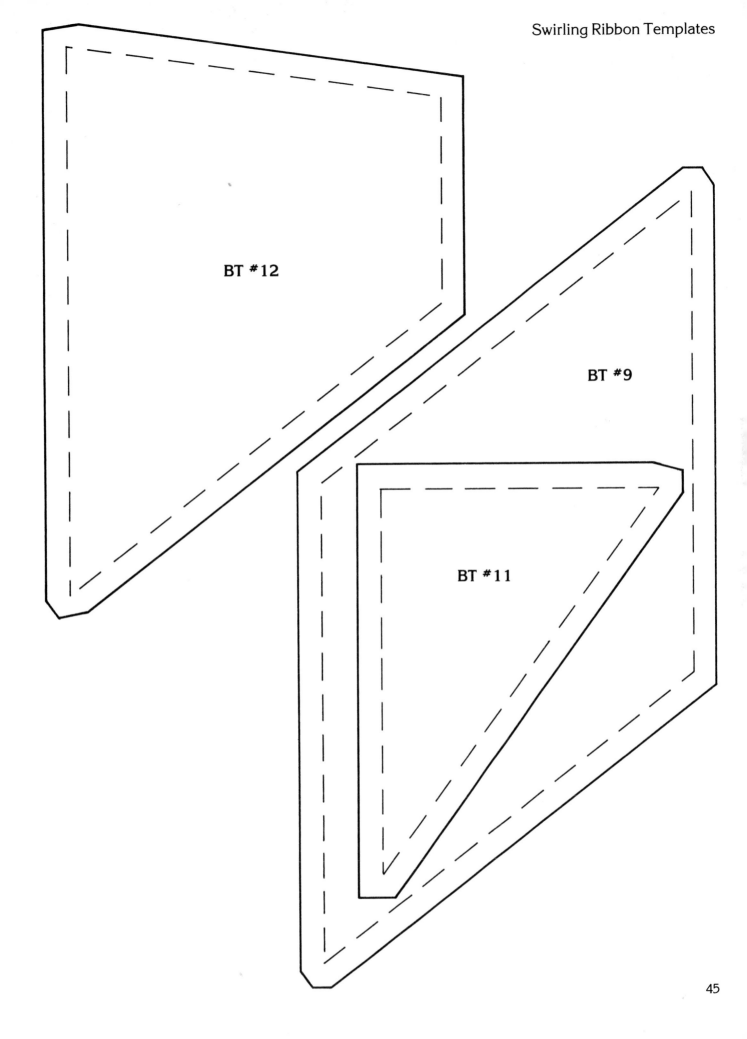

BT #12

BT #9

BT #11

INTERTWINING RIBBONS

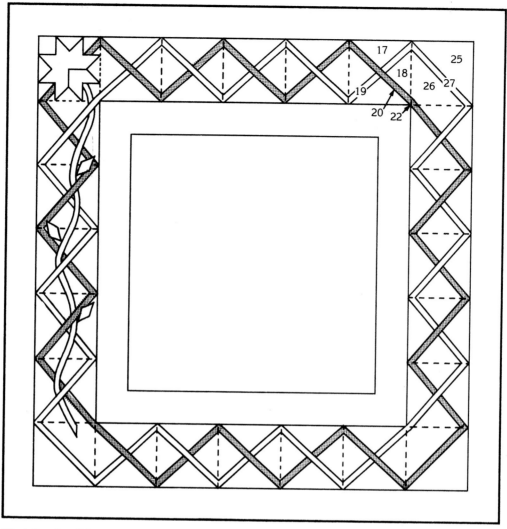

First Border #4

Intertwining Ribbons

This border pattern can be called airy. Its large open spaces seem to let light into your quilt as the "ribbons" twist and turn around its center. Adding the single peony in the corner was necessary to bring a little touch of blue to the outside edge. You could use a peony in each corner or repeat the ribbon corner 4 times, the choice is yours.

Even though this quilt has a feminine look of spring, this same border could be used in dark colors for a more masculine look.

To make the pink ribbon version I used, you will need to cut the following pieces:

Use BT #17, BT #18, BT #19, BT #20, BT #21, BT #22, BT #23, BT #24, BT #25, BT #26, BT #27, and MT A-8", MT B-8" and MT C-8"

From white —
Cut 40 BT #17   Cut 3 BT #25
Cut 40 BT #18   Cut 3 BT #26
Cut 1 BT #21   Cut 6 MT C-8"
Cut 2 BT #24   Cut 1 MT B-8"
Cut 4 frame strips 68" x 4 1/2"
Cut 4 binding strips 72" x 1 1/2"

From light pink —
Cut 20 BT #19
Cut 10 BT #20
Cut 2 BT #22
Cut 2 BT #27
From dark pink —
Cut 20 BT #19
Cut 10 BT #20
Cut 2 BT #22
Cut 2 BT #23
Cut 1 BT #27
From blue and pink-and-white print —
Cut 6 MT A-8"
From green leaf print —
Cut 2 MT A-8"
Cut several leaves
From green solid —
Cut 1 bias strip 1" x 45" for stem

PROCEDURE:

1. For the 8" peony corner block, construct background squares following diagram.

Make 2 Unit 1:

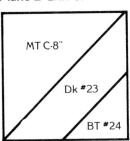

MT C-8"

Dk #23

BT #24

Make 1 Unit 2:

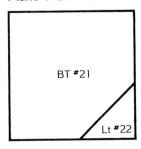

BT #21

Lt #22

2. Assemble 8" star block following diagram.

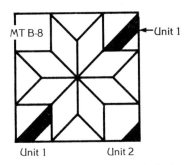

MT B-8 ← Unit 1

Unit 1   Unit 2

3. Construct 10 ribbon squares with dark pink #20 following diagram. These will be referred to as dark ribbon blocks.

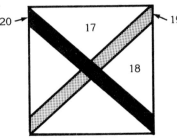

20 → 17 ← 19

18

4. Construct 10 ribbon squares with light pink #20. These will be referred to as light ribbon blocks.

20 → 17 ← 19

18

5. Construct 2 corner blocks with light pink #27 and dark pink #22.

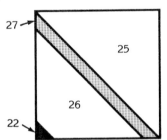

27 → 25

26

22 →

6. Construct 1 corner block with dark pink #27 and dark pink #22.

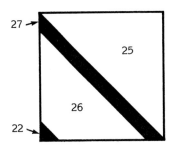

27 → 25

26

22 →

7. Construct 2 border strips, alternating 3 light and 2 dark ribbon blocks.

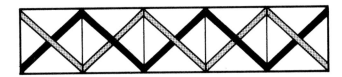

8. Construct 2 border strips, alternating 3 dark and 2 light ribbon blocks.

9. Stitch 2 identical border strips to opposite sides of center.

10. Join corner blocks to each end of the remaining border strips, matching light and dark ribbons.

11. Gently curve stem piece along 1 border strip. Rip a few stitches holding the ribbons in order to slide stem strip behind them.* Baste and applique leaves where desired.

12. Stitch border strips to remaining sides of quilt.

13. Add 4 frame strips and miter corners.

*To avoid having the dark stem show through a light ribbon, slip a small piece of white fabric between the seam allowances of the ribbon — making it twice as thick.

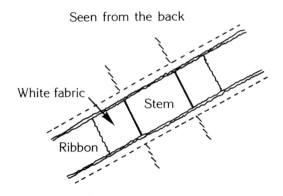

Seen from the back

White fabric

Stem

Ribbon

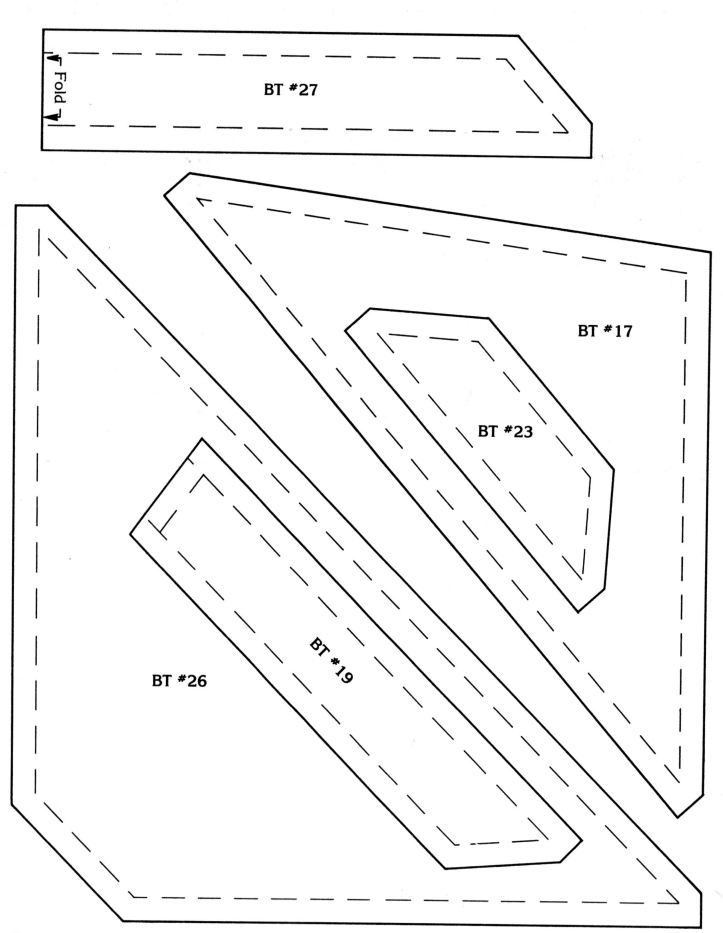

BT #27

Fold

BT #17

BT #23

BT #19

BT #26

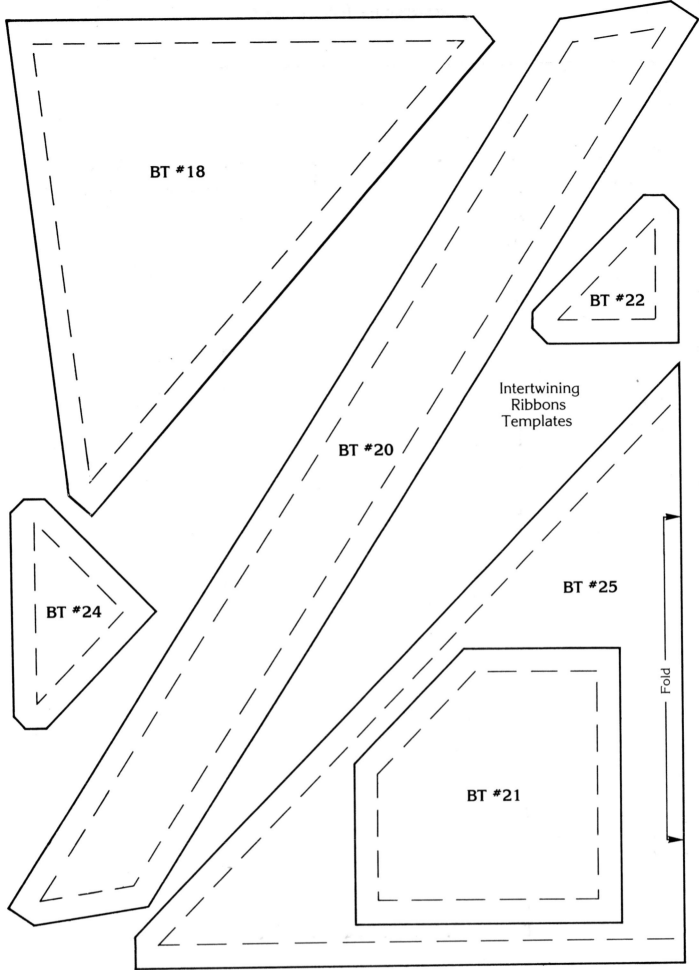

BT #18

BT #22

BT #20

Intertwining
Ribbons
Templates

BT #25

BT #24

Fold

BT #21

First Border #5   Philadelphia Pavement

This traditional pattern may be known to you by another name. There are many. Whatever people call it, they all agree it is lovely.

This version has been drafted to form rectangles of color in the corners. This would be an ideal place to embroider a message or quilt your name and the date.

If you are using the same colors I used to make the Pennsylvania Friendship quilt on page 18, you will have to cut the following pieces:

Use BT #15, BT #16
From light rose —
    Cut 48 BT #15
From dark rose —
    Cut 96 BT #15
From green —
    Cut 96 BT #16
From background —
    Cut 4 frame strips 68" x 4 1/2"
    Cut 4 binding strips 72" x 1 1/2"

PROCEDURE:

1. Construct 40 units following the diagram. You will use 10 units per side.

Note: Press the seams of each unit following the diagram. When joining units, the seams will automatically fit together.

2. Join 10 units to make each border strip.
3. Construct each of 4 corner units as follows:

    a. Stitch remaining squares and triangles into short strips.

    b. Join short strips to form triangles.

4. Stitch corner unit to end of each border strip.

5. To save extra steps, center frame strips and stitch to long side of border strip.
6. Attach border strips to quilt center and miter frame strips and border strips in one step.

Philadelphia Pavement Templates

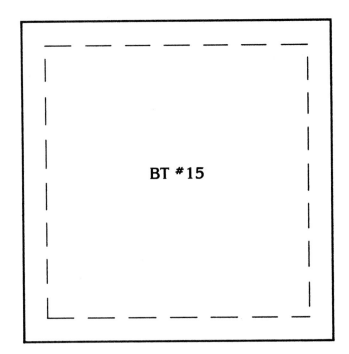

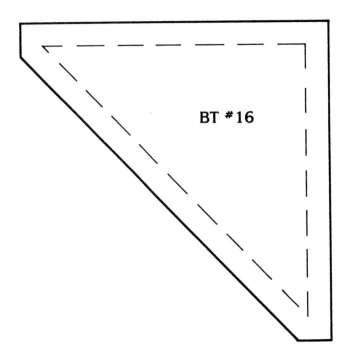

DRESDEN BLOSSOMS

First Border #6

Dresden Blossoms

Many times simply repeating a traditional block design can make a lovely border. Here the Dresden Plate was used in alternating 8" units with gently curving stems and leaves. It was combined with the Baskets and Butterflies center to make the purple quilt shown on page 78. What a wonderful scrap quilt it would make.

If you are coloring your border as I colored mine, you will have to cut the following pieces:

Use BT #28, BT #29, and BT #30

From dark purple solid —
    Cut 2 strips 40 1/2" x 8 1/2"
    Cut 2 strips 56 1/2" x 8 1/2"
    Cut 4 frame strips 68" x 4 1/2"
    Cut 4 binding strips 72" x 1 1/2"

From each of 8 different pink and purple solids —
    Cut 12 BT #28
From green print —
    Cut 12 BT #29
    Cut 28 BT #30
    Cut 12 yards bias strips 1" wide

PROCEDURE:

1.   For each of 12 blossoms, join 8 blossom pieces to construct flower. Press seams open.

2.   Press under outside edges 1/4" using paper pressing template to assure nice curve.

3.   Gather center circle around paper circle pressing template and press.

4.   Center green circle on blossoms and applique.

5.   Prepare large strips for applique; measure border strips in 8" sections and mark by creasing with a iron. Note -- end blocks are 8 1/4".

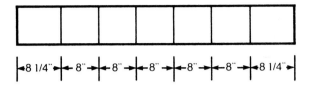

6.   Lay creased strip over stem placement diagram and transfer all markings to the fabric.

7.   Prepare stem strips for applique by turning under 1/4" along each edge and basting.

8.   Prepare leaves for applique by pressing around pressing template and basting along each edge.

9.   Baste green stems and leaves in place on border strip. When basting stems on 40" strip, baste to within 4" of seam to leave end free for stitching seam.

10.   Applique leaves and stems.

11.   Baste 2 blossoms to each border strip between stem pieces.

12.   Stitch each short border strip to opposite sides of quilt center.

13.   Stitch long border strips to the remaining 2 sides of center.

14.   Finish appliqueing stems over border seams.

15.   Applique 1 of the remaining blossoms to each corner.

16.   Applique last 4 leaves over the corner of the first frame strips.

17.   Stitch last frame strip to quilt and miter corners.

Dresden Blossoms Templates

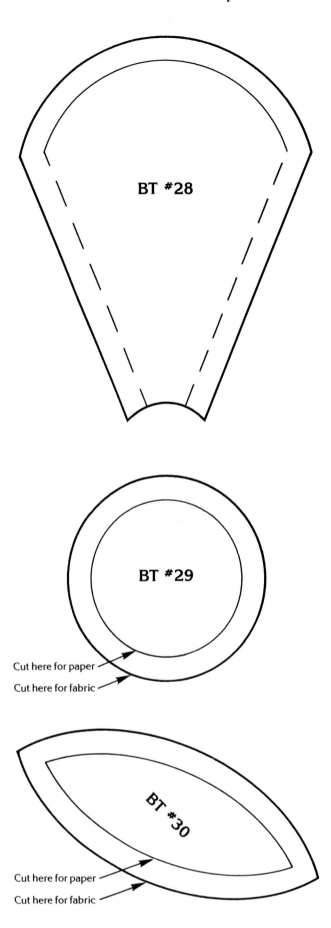

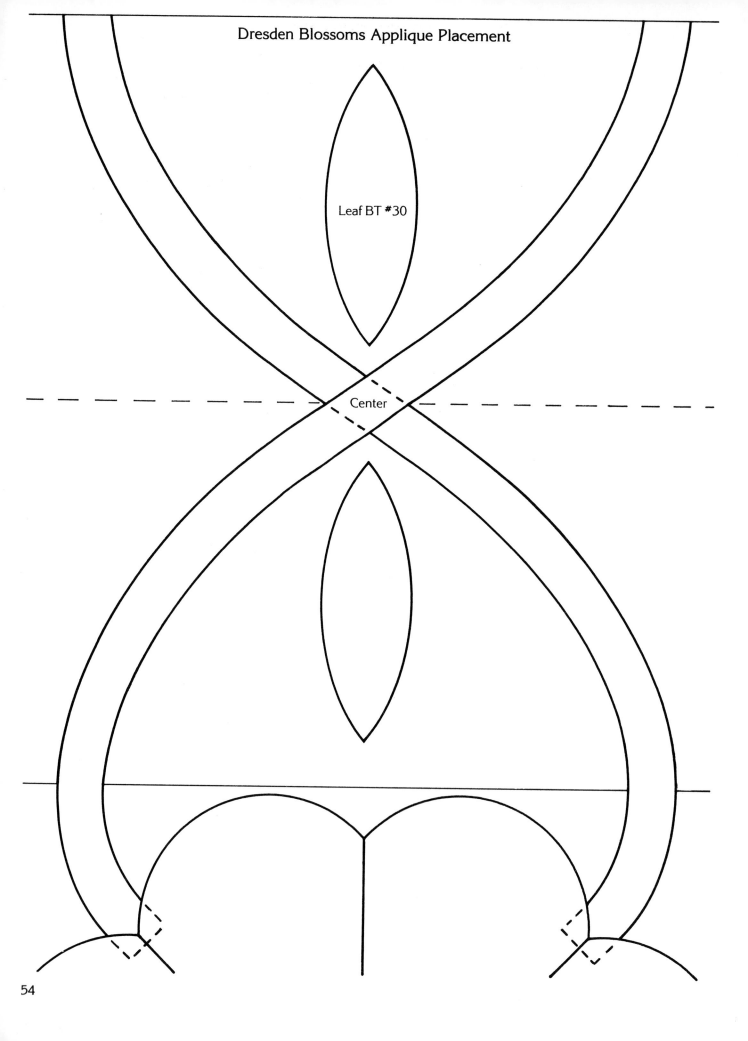

Dresden Blossoms Applique Placement

Leaf BT #30

Center

First Border #7   Purely Quilting

Sometimes a center design is so lovely by itself that to add a pieced border would detract from it. This border of beautiful quilting will enhance any center design.

PROCEDURE:

1. Make a photocopy of the corner quilting design, and 4 copies of the side border design. Tape the copies together and darken lines if necessary.

2. Cut 4 strips 60" x 8 1/2".

3. Join frame strips to each border strip.

4. Stitch border strips to quilt center. Miter border strip and frame strip in 1 step.

5. Center quilting pattern under border strip. Transfer designs to border strip.

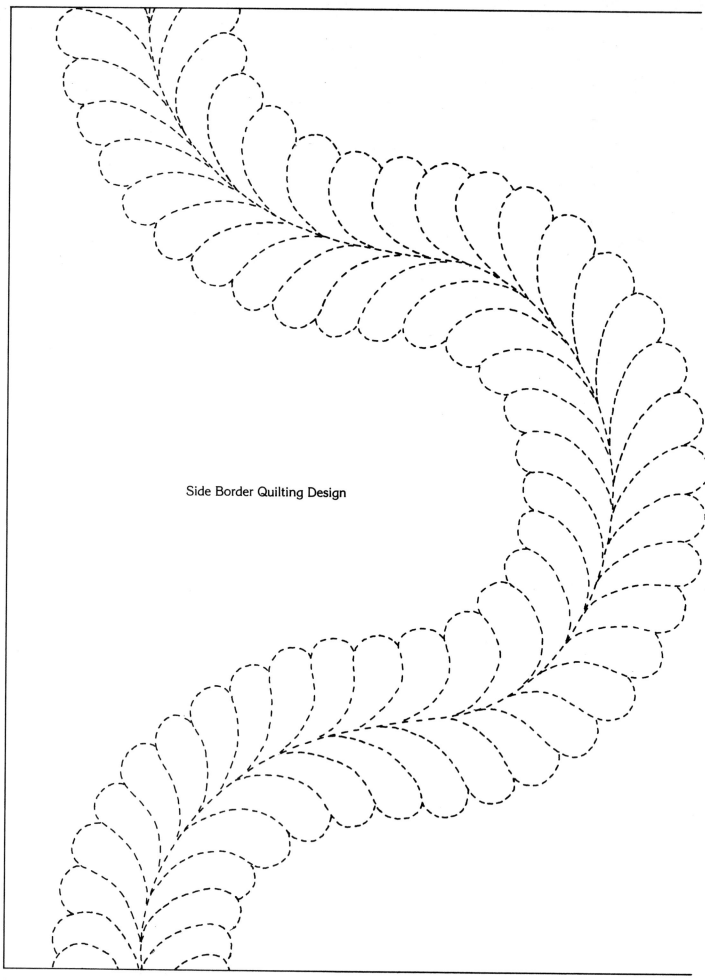

Side Border Quilting Design

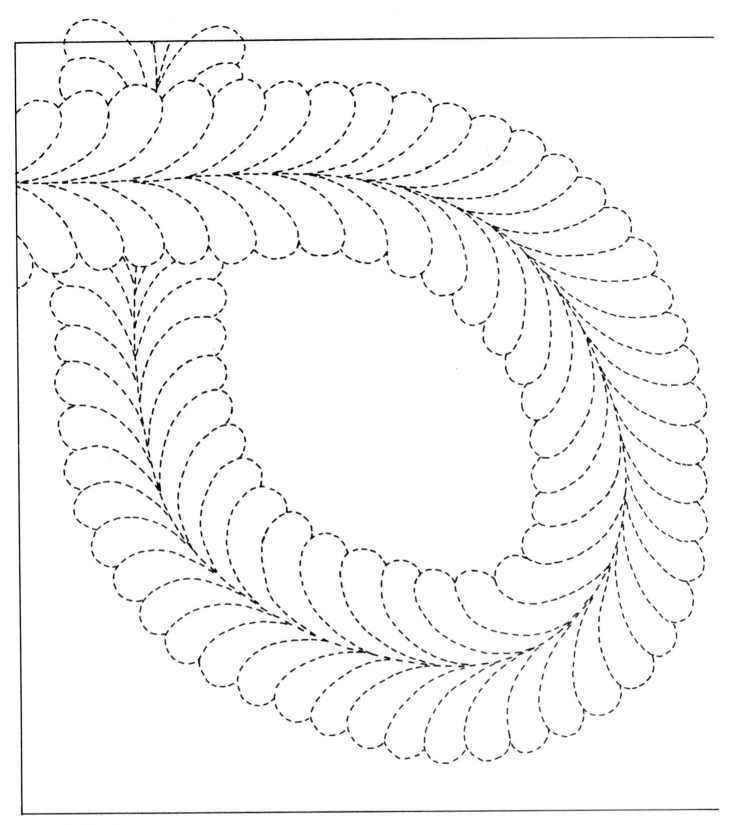

Corner Quilting Design

CALCULATING STARS AND OCTAGONS

If you have completed your quilt center, you now have a better understanding of the three basic shapes of a star and how they relate to each other. When planning a very large center pattern, and particularly when planning an octagonal border, it becomes necessary to tape many large pieces of graph paper together to draft the 64" design or figure the shape using algebra. Using simple math calculations is far more accurate and not so difficult as we have been led to believe.

The side of the basic star square is divided into three sections.

Two of the sections (A) are equal. Section B is 1.414 times the length of A. The number 1.414 is used because it is the square root of 2. (Don't read the next two sentences if you are already confused.) If you assign the value of 1 to each leg of the right angle, then using the Pythagorean theorem, add the squares of the 2 numbers. $(1 \times 1) + (1 \times 1) = 2$. The square root of 2 is the length of the long side of the triangle. No matter what size square you are working with, section B will always be 1.414 times the length of section A. Thank you Pythagoras.

Section A	Section B	Section A

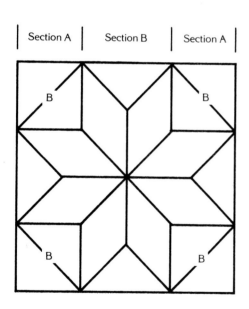

To find the length of A and B, use an equation to find two unknowns. Let's use a 32" square as an example. (Measurements for all the block sizes in the Master Template section are on page 59.)

2A + B = 32
2A + (1.414)A = 32 (Remember B= A x 1.414)
2A + 1.414 A = 32 (Add together)
3.414 A = 32
A = 32 ÷ 3.414 or 3.414)32‾
A = 9.373
B = 9.373 x 1.414
B = 13.253

You now know the length of each of the three sections of the side of the 32" square. The length of B is equal to the length of each side of a 32" octagon.

Use the length of B to determine the frame strips for the octagon center.

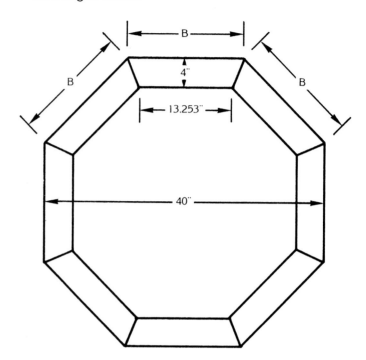

By adding 4" frames the octagon is now based on a 40" square. Use the same calculation to find the outside measurement.

2A + B = 40"
2A + (1.414)A = 40
2A + 1.414 A = 40
3.414 A = 40
A = 40 ÷ 3.414A = 11.716
B = 11.716 x 1.414
B = 16.567

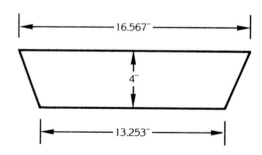

When both outside lengths are known, it is a simple process to center the smaller figure 4" under the larger figure and connect the end points of each line to complete the drawing. Decimals are not a problem if you use 10 squares-to-the-inch graph paper. It is automatically divided into 10ths; the 100ths fall between the lines.

To add the first border, repeat the same equation using a 56" square as the base.

$$2A + B = 56$$
$$2A + (1.414)A = 56$$
$$2A + 1.414\ A = 56$$
$$3.414\ A = 56$$

$$A = 56 \div 3.414$$
$$A = 16.403$$
$$B = 16.403 \times 1.414$$
$$B = 23.194$$

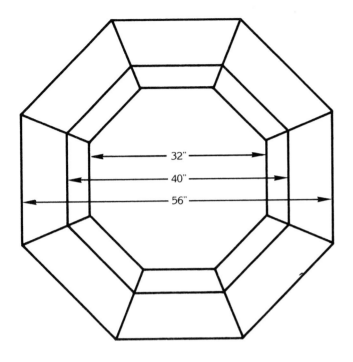

This piece is very large and now off the edge of the paper. It is necessary to draw only one-half of it to have the template you need. Simply reverse the template and draw the second half on your material.

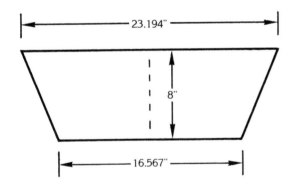

The last border strip is 4" wide. Repeat the calculation to find its outside edge using a 64" square as a reference.

$$2A + B = 64$$
$$2A + (1.414)A = 64$$
$$2A + 1.414\ A = 64$$
$$3.414\ A = 64$$
$$A = 64 \div 3.414$$
$$A = 18.746$$
$$B = 18.746 \times 1.414$$
$$B = 26.507$$

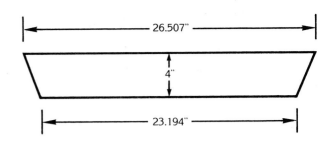

I have used the 32" square for the example because that is what we are working with for these quilts. The following measurements are for each square in the Master Templates section rounded off to the nearest 1000th:

32" square	A = 9.373" B = 13.253"	8" square	A = 2.343" B = 3.313"
24" square	A = 7.029" B = 9.940"	6" square	A = 1.757" B = 2.485"
16" square	A = 4.686" B = 6.626"	4" square	A = 1.171" B = 1.656"
12" square	A = 3.514" B = 4.970"	3" square	A = .878" B = 1.242"

If you are uncomfortable using decimals, convert them to fractions using the following chart. Remember these have been rounded off to the nearest 1000th. The small amount of inaccuracy you may experience due to rounding off is probably equal to less than the difference in your pieces when you use a sharp pencil versus a very sharp pencil to trace the shape on your material.

.0625	= 1/16"	.5625	= 9/16"
.0833	= 1/12"	.5833	= 7/12"
.1	= 1/10"	.6	= 3/5"
.1250	= 1/8"	.625	= 5/8"
.1666	= 1/6"	.6666	= 2/3"
.1875	= 3/16"	.6875	= 11/16"
.2	= 1/5"	.7	= 7/10"
.25	= 1/4"	.75	= 3/4"
.3	= 3/10"	.8	= 4/5"
.3125	= 5/16"	.8125	= 13/16"
.3333	= 1/3"	.8333	= 5/6"
.375	= 3/8"	.875	= 7/8"
.4	= 2/5"	.9	= 9/10"
.4166	= 5/12"	.9166	= 11/12"
.4375	= 7/16"	.9375	= 15/16"
.5	= 1/2"		

BORDERING OCTAGONS

Working with octagons is always fun. They have a totally different look and are no more difficult to make than squares. In this basic layout, you will be fitting a square around an octagon.

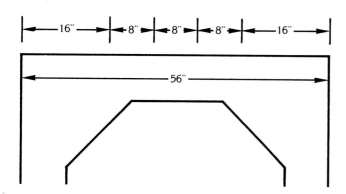

To fulfill the basic requirement of a 56" border, the side has been divided into three 8" squares. The corner can then be filled with a 16" eight-pointed star that has been altered by replacing one of its corner squares with one more of its side triangles. It would seem logical that the slightly altered 16" 8-pointed star block would fit perfectly in the corner of the border, but, IT DOES NOT. A very narrow strip must be stitched to the four sides of your octagon that will be next to your corner squares. This strip is labeled filler template #1. Filler template #2 is used to fill the small space between the large and small blocks, next to the octagon.

The basic layout is the border pattern I used to make the Preppy Medallion on page 80. If you are coloring yours the way I colored mine, you will have to cut the following pieces: Use MT A-8", MT B-8", MT C-8", MT A-16", MT B-16", MT C-16" and filler templates #1 and #2.

From red solid —
    Cut 64 MT A-8"
From red print —
    Cut 32 MT A-8"
From navy print —
    Cut 32 MT A-16"
From tan —
    Cut 48 MT B-8"
    Cut 48 MT C-8"
    Cut 12 MT B-16"
    Cut 20 MT C-16"
    Cut 8 FT #2
    Cut 4 FT #1
From stripe —
    Cut 4 frame strips 68" x 4 1/2"
    Cut 4 binding strips 72" x 1 1/2"

PROCEDURE:
1.   Construct 8 of the 8" 8-pointed star blocks, using red solid with tan background.

2.   Construct 4 of the 8" 8-pointed star blocks, using red print with tan background.

3.   Make 4 strips of 3 star blocks each, alternating solid, print, and solid stars.

4.   Construct 4 navy blue 16" 8-pointed star blocks with tan background, following diagram. (Replace corner squares with triangles.)

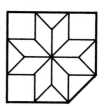

5.   Stitch 4 filler strips to alternate sides of octagon.

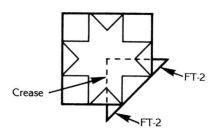

6.   Fold 16" star in half and crease side triangles to determine placement of filler triangles #2.

7.   Join 2 filler triangles to 2 sides of star.

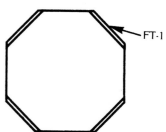

8.   Join corner square to octagon along filler strips.

9.   Set in side strips.

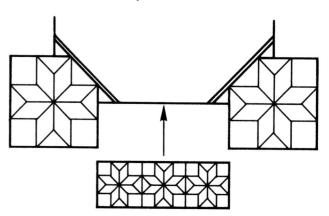

10.   Add frame strips and miter corners. See mitering instructions on page 94.

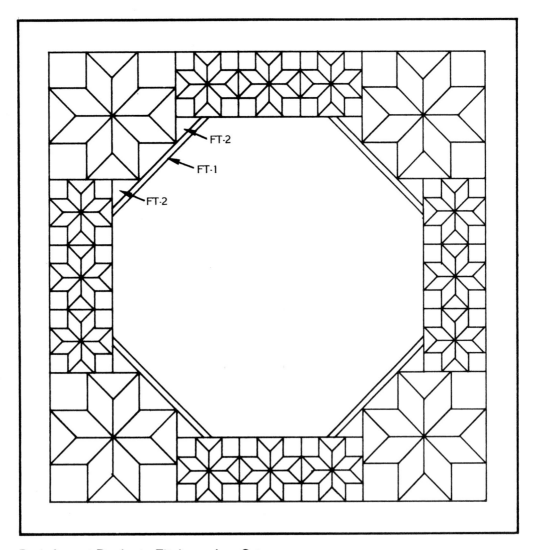

Basic Layout Border to Fit Around an Octagon

There are an infinite number of ways to change the basic layout using the master templates. The 16" squares in the corners could be replaced with any of the octagonal 16" patterns. Remember, those are any of the 32" center patterns made with MT 16" and designated as being able to be made into an octagon.

The 8" squares along the sides of the border can be replaced with 8" pieced blocks made with MT 8" or MT 4". As an example, should you want to repeat the 32" center pattern in an 8" block, use the master templates that have the same proportions. A 32" pattern made with master templates from the 16" block section can be reproduced in an 8" square using 4" templates. (Sixteen is one-half of thirty-two so use the templates that are one-half of 8" to make a square of the same design.)

Maybe you want only one 8" pieced block along the side. Replace the two extra star blocks with two solid squares. Actually, any pattern could be substituted as long as its finished size is 8".

You could also fill in the 8" x 24" side area by putting one-half of a 16" block in the center. This would require one more filler template. It is provided and marked filler template #3. It is the rectangle required to fill the half square left by placing a 16" half block in the center of the 24" space.

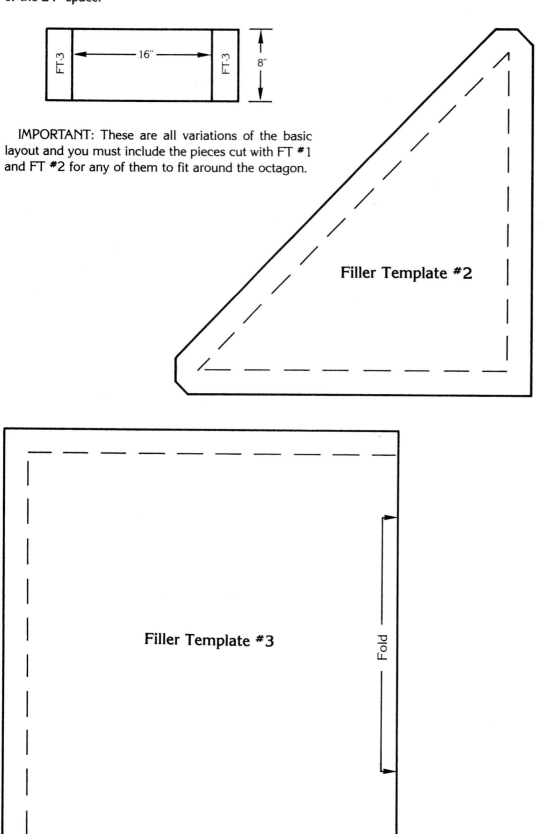

IMPORTANT: These are all variations of the basic layout and you must include the pieces cut with FT #1 and FT #2 for any of them to fit around the octagon.

Filler Template #2

Filler Template #3

Filler Template #1

OCTAGONAL BORDER

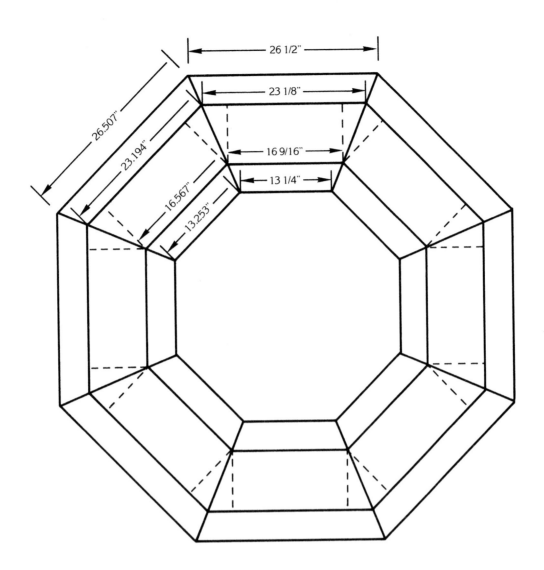

It is possible to surround your center octagon with another octagon. The basic shape on each side of the octagon is shown here.

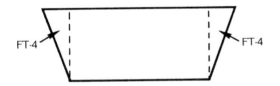

A 16" x 8" rectangle fits well here. Filler template #4 is the piece used to fill out the basic shape. Remember to cut one up and one reversed for each of the eight sides. Half 16" squares could be used to fill the octagon or two 8" squares or eight 4" squares.

Of course, you could always make your own solid template by drawing a 16" x 8" rectangle and tracing filler template #4 on each side. Think of the wonderful applique you could twist and turn around the center octagon.

PIECED OCTAGONAL BORDERS

Any square or rectangular border can be adapted to serve as an octagonal border. The simplest method would be to make 8 short pieced panels and trim the ends, using the slanted edge of Filler Template #4 as a guide. By carefully centering the same design motif in the middle of each panel, you will be assured that the patchwork pieces along each seam will match exactly and look perfectly mitered.

It is also possible to redraw any of the border patterns to create your own interesting corner treatment. Use the figures on the diagram to draw the actual size border section; then add the grid of your choice.

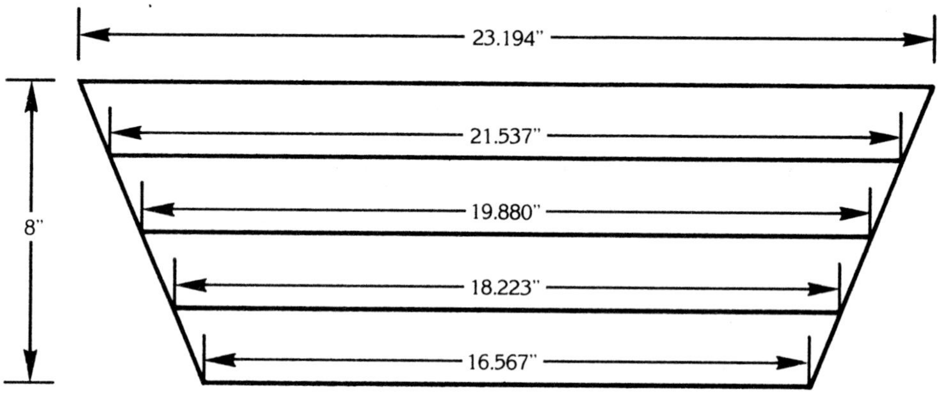

Filler Template #4

23.194"
21.537"
19.880"
18.223"
16.567"
8"

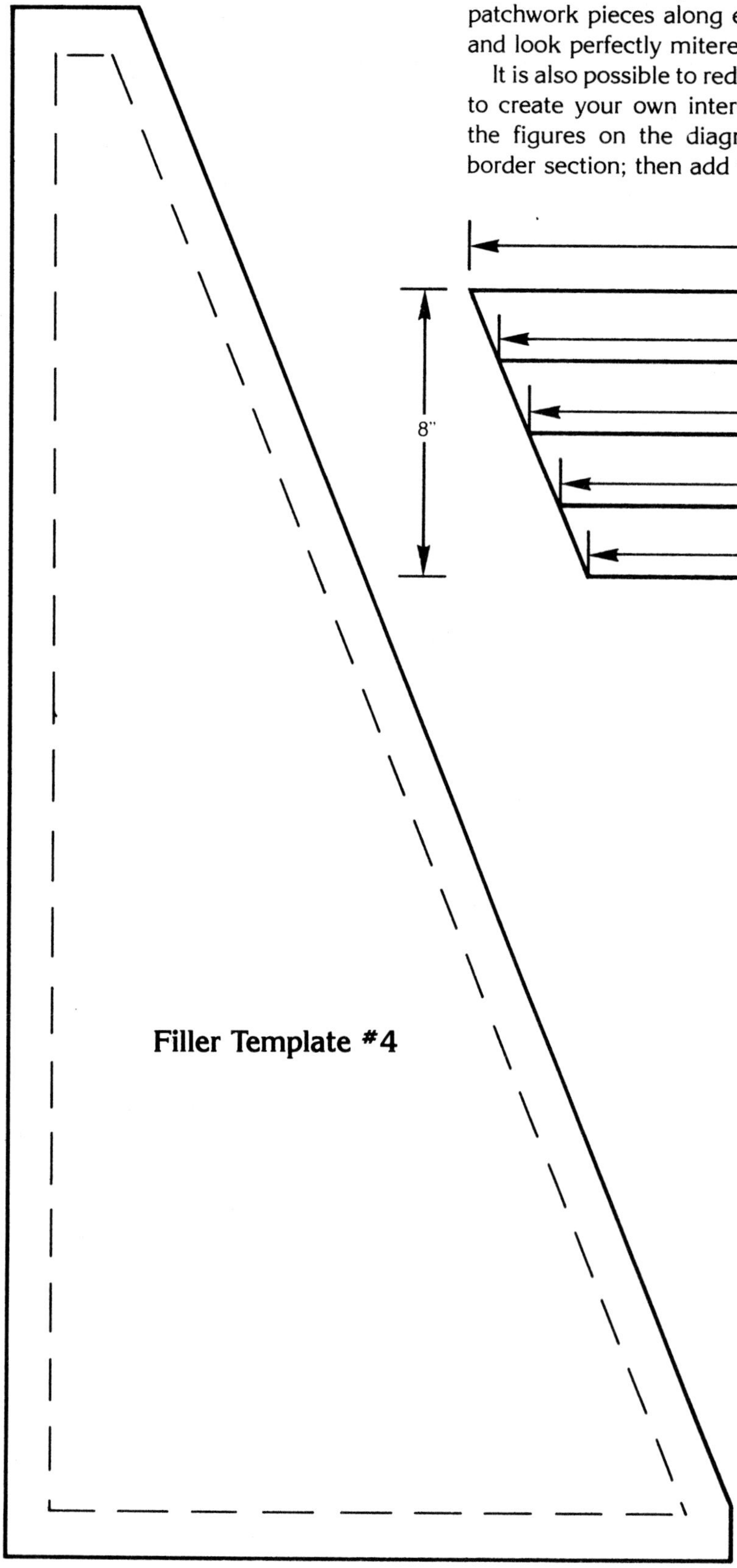

SECOND BORDERS

These borders are designed to fit around the first borders and frame strips. They are all 8" wide and 80" long. These borders make up the portion of your quilt that will be hanging off the edge of the bed.

Like the first borders, many of these patterns are designed in 8", 4", or 2" increments. Several of the patterns can be made to fit as first borders by subtracting some of the units.

Always check an altered pattern by tracing it and checking its placement on the master grid.

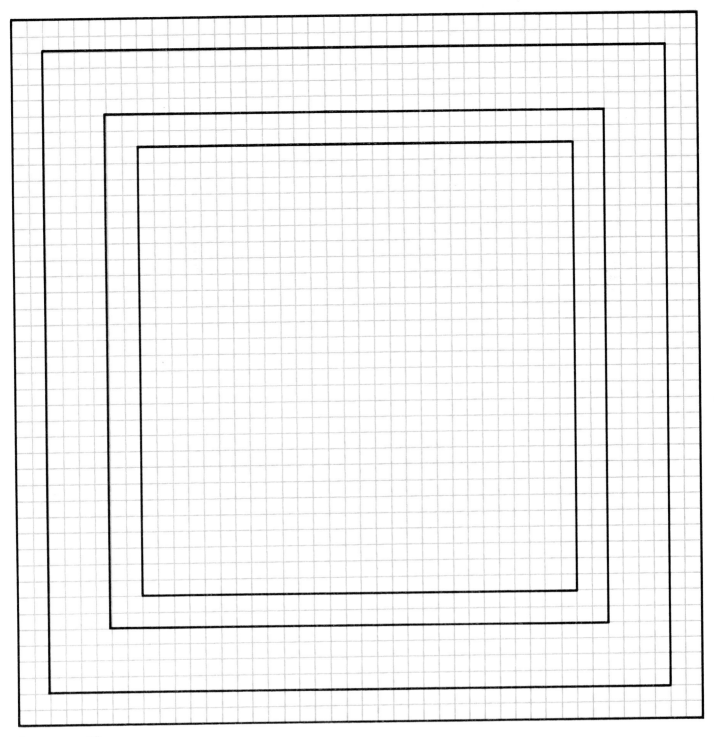

1 square = 2"

MASTER GRID

This is the basic layout of the second border. Lay tracing paper over the grid and draw your original design. Use this grid to test an enlarged pattern from the first border section.

ARGYLE

Second Border #1

Argyle

What could be more fun than an argyle quilt. Look at a few sweaters for suggestions on how to color this border. The border can appear to float around the center if you make the outside triangles from the same fabric as the frame strips. If the triangles are made from a contrasting fabric, the border will have a very solid look.

This border is made from repeated 8" blocks. You will need to make thirty-six for the outside border. To use this design for an inside border, you will need to make twenty-four blocks. The number of pieces you cut

from each fabric will depend on how you have colored the border. Use BT #31, BT #32, BT #33, and BT #34.

PROCEDURE:

1. Assemble each block by making 4 triangles. Each triangle is made by joining 2 triangles #34 to 2 sides of #33.

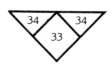

66

Argyle Border Templates

BT #32

BT #34

BT #33

BT #31

2. Stitch 2 triangle units to each side of #31, twice.

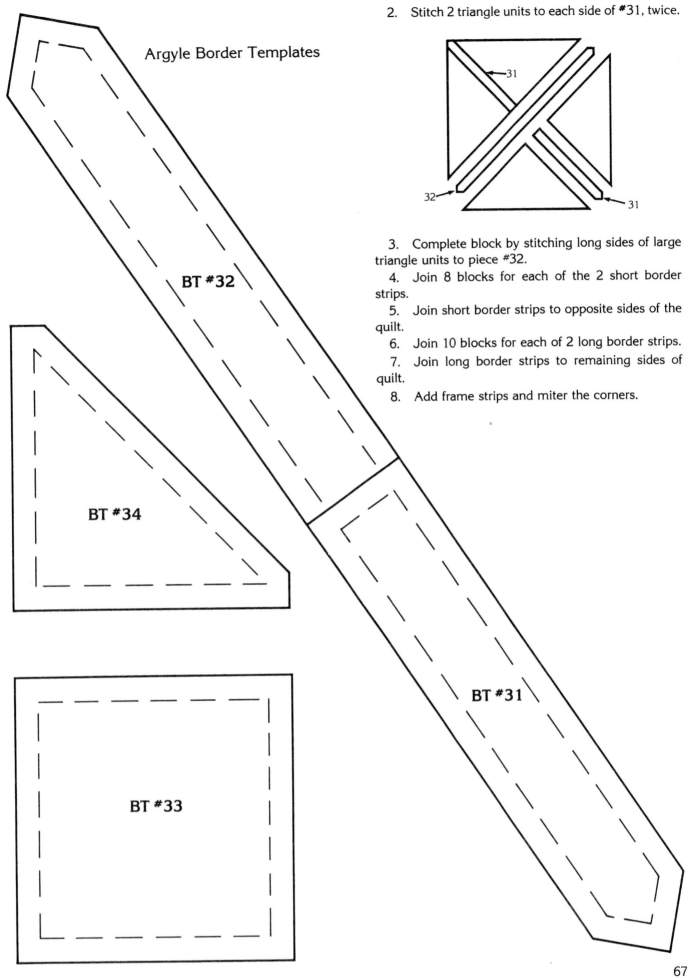

31

32

31

3. Complete block by stitching long sides of large triangle units to piece #32.

4. Join 8 blocks for each of the 2 short border strips.

5. Join short border strips to opposite sides of the quilt.

6. Join 10 blocks for each of 2 long border strips.

7. Join long border strips to remaining sides of quilt.

8. Add frame strips and miter the corners.

Second Border #2

Album

A friendship quilt needs to be signed by all of its makers. This album patch border provides the perfect place for signatures. This border is based on the repeat of an 8" square so it is suitable for the inner or outer border. Use BT #35, BT #36, BT #37, BT #38, BT #39, and BT #40.

PROCEDURE:

1. Join pieces in strips.

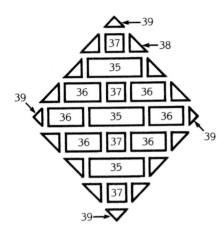

2. Join strips and add triangles to complete 36 blocks.

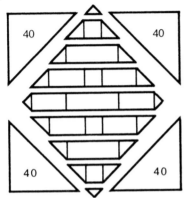

3. Construct 2 short border strips by joining 8 blocks for each.

4. Stitch the 2 short border strips to opposite sides of the quilt.

5. Construct 2 long border strips by joining 10 blocks for each.

6. Stitch 2 remaining sides of the quilt.

7. Join frame strips and miter corners.

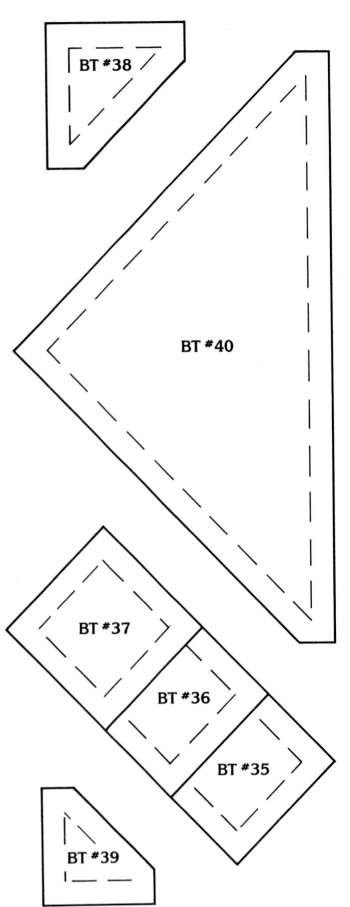

BT #38

BT #40

BT #37

BT #36

BT #35

BT #39

Second Border #3   Bethlehem Blossom

This border seems to repeat the Bethlehem Rose blossom. It would be equally lovely around many of the centers.

It is easily constructed from thirty-six identical 8" blocks. It is suitable as a first border, but you must change the direction of the blocks. Work it out on graph paper before you make a final decision.

To color this border the way I have in the Bethlehem Rose Medallion shown on page 79, you will need to cut the following pieces: BT #42, BT #43, BT #44, and BT #45.

CUTTING:
    From medium peach print —
        Cut 72 BT #42
    From light peach print —
        Cut 36 BT #43
    From rust print —
        Cut 36 BT #44
        Cut 36 BT #44 reversed
    From beige background —
        Cut 36 BT #45

PROCEDURE: To construct each of 36 blocks:

1. Join 2 #42s on short side.
2. Set in #43 square.
3. Set in 2 #44s on remaining sides of square #43.
4. Complete block by joining #45.
5. Join 8 blocks to form each of 2 border strips. Reverse direction of block at center of strip.
6. Stitch strips to opposite sides of quilt center.
7. Join 10 blocks to form each of 2 long border strips. Reverse direction of blocks at center.
8. Join long strips to remaining sides of quilt.
9. Add frame strips and miter corners.

Bethlehem Blossom Templates

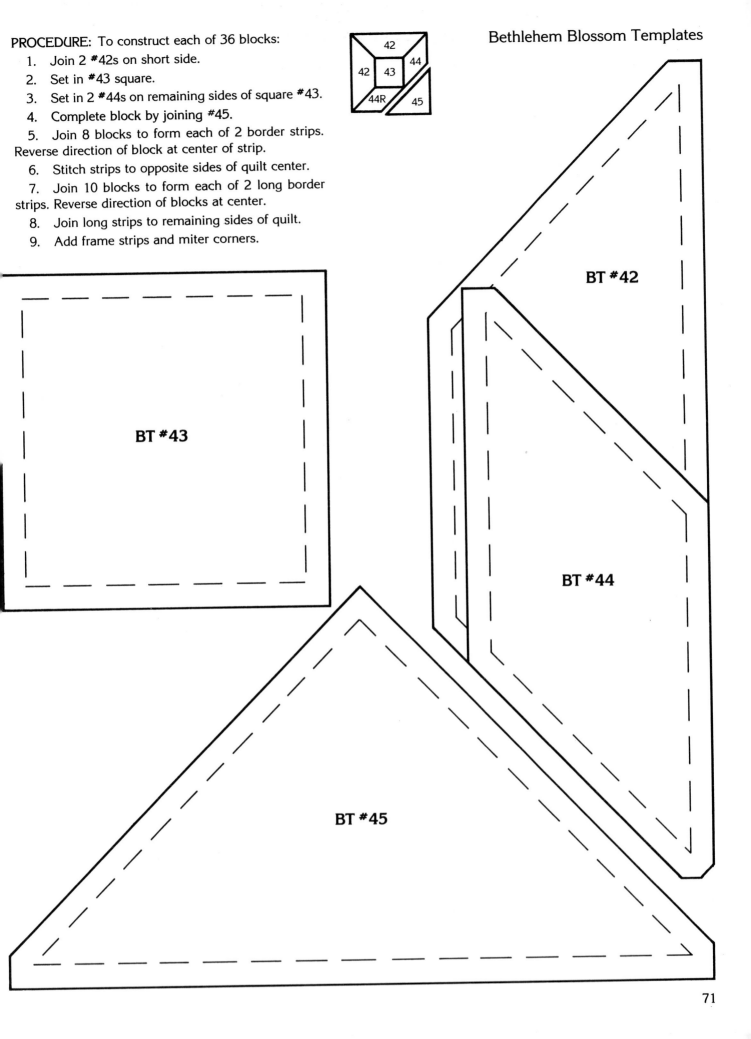

BT #43

BT #42

BT #44

BT #45

Second Border #4

Accordian

This border can be bold or light depending on how you use the colors. It is based on a 4" repeat so it is possible to use it as a first border by using fewer repeats. Be sure to work the design on graph paper before you make a final decision to use it as a first border.

Remember to reverse the template on half of the BT #46 pieces.

Use BT #46, BT #47, BT #48, BT #49, BT #50, and BT #51.

PROCEDURE:

1. Join 2 triangles #47 to each end of #46 to form a rectangular unit.

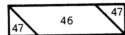

2. Join 32 rectangular units to form 2 short border strips.

3. Join 2 short border strips to opposite sides of quilt center.

4. To construct each of 4 corner squares:
Join 1 piece #47 to 1 angled side of #48, #49, and #50. Repeat for reversed #48, #49, and #50. Join to form triangle.

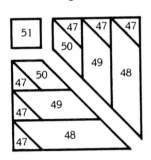

Join triangles on long edge. Set in square #51.

5. Join 1 corner square to each end of remaining border strips.

6. Join border strips to remaining sides of quilt.

7. Add frame strips and miter corners.

Accordian Border Templates

BT #50

BT #49

BT #51

BT #46

BT #48

BT #47

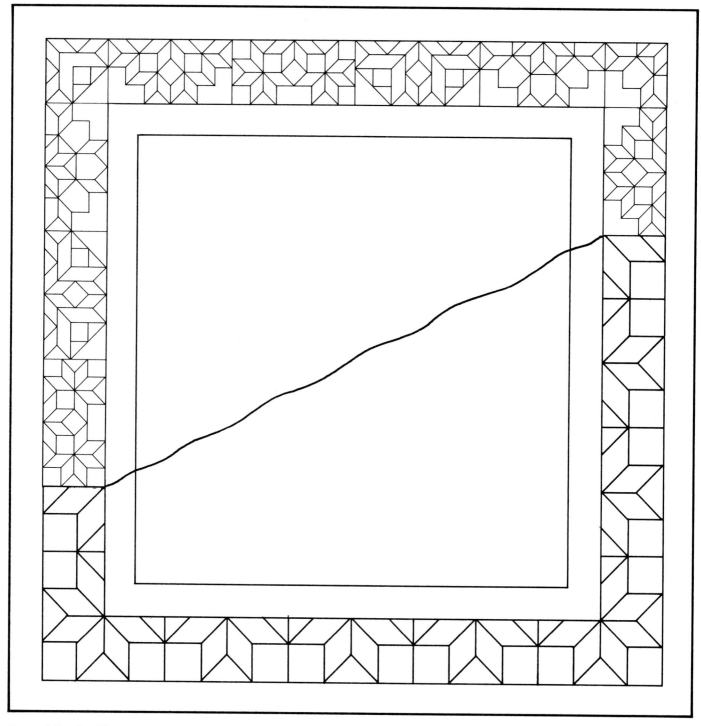

Second Border #5

Half Stars

Because the border area is eight inches wide it is possible to use repeats of one-half 16" blocks to border your center block. If you have designed your own 32" center use the templates that are one-half the size of the ones you used to make the block.

The way you set the half stars will affect the final look of the quilt. Most of the star patterns form circles of color. If you turn the half stars so that they point to the center of your quilt, the patterns will form a design that is similar to that in the top portion of the drawing. Notice that there are four half blocks on each side and one quarter of a block in each corner.

By turning the half squares so that they point away from the center of the quilt, the effect will be much different (see lower portion of the drawing). In this arrangement, each side is now made of three half blocks. Three-fourths of a square is needed to fill out each corner.

Because this border forms the portion of the quilt that will be hanging down the side of the bed, consider how each arrangement will look from the side before you make your final decision.

WILD GOOSE CHASE

Second Border #6

Wild Goose Chase

One of the options not yet explored is to divide the border horizontally. All of the previous borders have been designed in 8", 4", or 2" increments. By subtracting 1" from each side of the 8" border strip, it is possible to use designs based on 6" and 3". Two 1" strips are used to add contrast and maintain the same proportions used in the first borders.

Use BT #52, BT #53, BT #54, and BT #55.

CUTTING:

For each segment —
    Cut 1 BT #52
    Cut 2 BT #53

For each corner block —
    Cut 1 BT #54
    Cut 1 BT #55 from the same fabric as BT #54
    Cut 3 BT #55 from background fabric

Also —
    Cut 4 strips 70" x 1 1/2" from contrast
    Cut 4 strips 82" x 1 1/2" from contrast
    Cut 4 frame strips 92" x 4 1/2"

PROCEDURE:

1. Join 2BT #53 to each BT #52 to form segment.

2. Join 22 segments to make each of 4 border units.

3. Construct corner blocks by following diagram.

4. Join short 1 1/2" border strips to quilt and miter corners.

5. Join the 2 border units to opposite sides of quilt center.

6. Stitch 1 corner block to each end of remaining border units.

7. Join long pieced border units to remaining sides of quilt.

8. Stitch last 1 1/2" border strip to last frame strip. Join to quilt and miter both in one step.

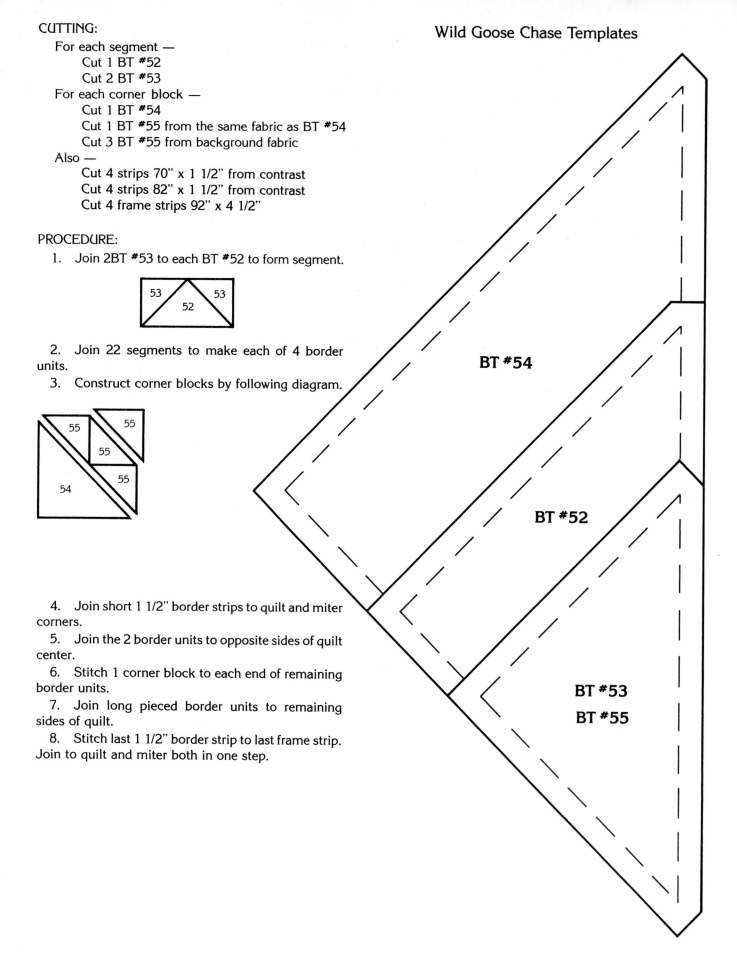

The Christmas Medallion Quilt, 64" x 64", captures the holiday mood with its Carpenter's Wheel center and Overlapping Diamonds border. Co-ordinating 16" pillows are made using the 8" templates for the center designs: the Poinsettia pillow has yellow centers added to the Lone Star block; Peony pillow quilted by Kathie Connolly; Carpenter's Wheel and Maple Leaf pillow quilted by Carola Blankenbeckler. Avoid losing star points on pillows by bordering the block with a 1 1/2" strip of fabric.

This vibrant **Basket and Butterflies Quilt,** 64" x 64", uses eight shades of pink and lavender set against a purple background. The gentle curves of the Dresden Blossom border provide a nice contrast to the sharp angles of the center design. **The Basket and Butterflies Scrap Quilt,** 54" x 69", by Muriel McLean is a variation of the pattern. The 12" Basket and Butterfly blocks are set together with solid blue lattice.

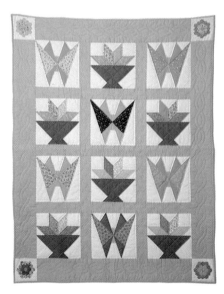

The Bethlehem Rose Quilt, 88" x 88", provides a stunning focal point for the bedroom. Coordinating pillow shams, a pleated dust ruffle, and a companion Blue and Blue Star wall quilt complete the total look; the Blue and Blue Star wall quilt has nine 16" stars made in alternating colors.

A unique octagonal border surrounds the Star of Magi center in the **Preppie Medallion Quilt,** 64¨ x 64¨. Named for the striped cotton print which reminds one of men's ties, the **Preppie Medallion Quilt** will brighten any room. The tan fabric makes an effective background for the striped borders and pieced stars. Balance is achieved by repeating the blue print in the corner stars of the same size.

BEN'S WANDERING DUCK FOOT

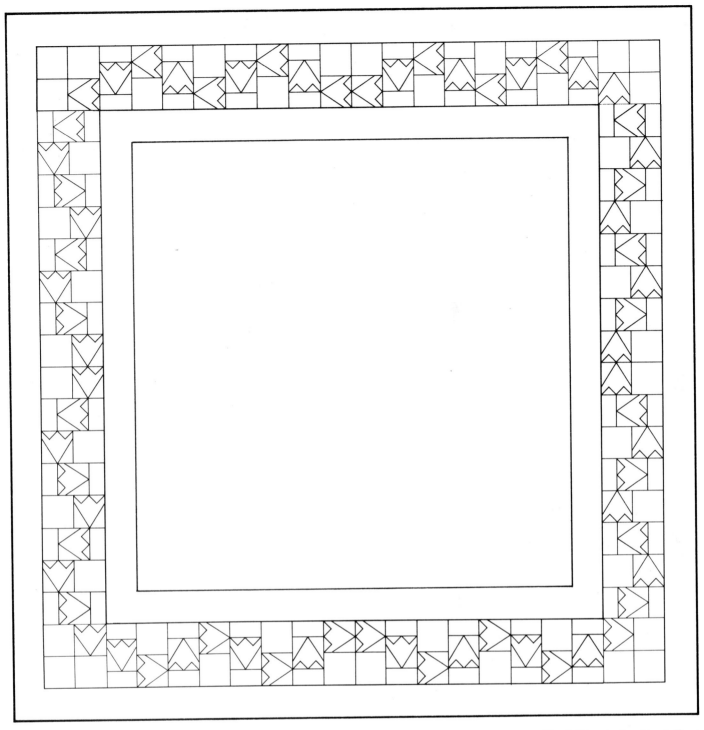

Second Border #7

Ben's Wandering Duck Foot

Just as I try to show an interest in my husband's garage full of "wonderful things," he tries to show an interest in my quilting activities. I go to junk yards with him; he goes to quilt shows with me. Therefore, I was not totally surprised when one evening he looked over my shoulder at my doodles and said, "I know that one, it's a 'Wandering Duck Foot'." So much enthusiasm cannot go unrewarded. So, here in honor of my husband is Ben's Wandering Duck Foot.

This border illustrates how easily any 4" pattern can be made to ramble around the width of the 8" border. Joining each pieced 4" block to a 4" background square or two 4" x 2" rectangles causes the design to flow up and down the border space. If 4" star blocks replaced the feet, they might look like shooting stars. Try a few of your favorites and see what you come up with.

1. For each of the sixty-eight pieced blocks required, you will need to cut the following:

From motif fabric —
    1 BT #57
    2 BT #58
    1 BT #59

From background fabric —
    1 BT #56
    1 BT #56 reversed
    2 BT #59

2. From background fabric, cut 48 4" squares, using BT #65.

3. Cut 64 rectangles using BT #64.

PROCEDURE:

1. Assemble each of 68 pieced blocks following the diagram.

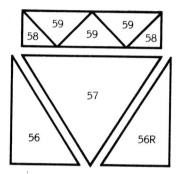

2. For each of 16 units #1, join square #61 to pieced block, following diagram.

3. For each of 16 units #2, join square #61 to pieced block, following diagram.

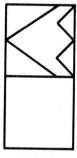

Unit #1   Unit #2

4. For each of 32 units #3, join 2 rectangles #60 to pieced block, following diagram.

Unit #3

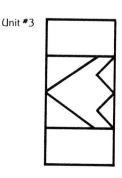

5. Join remaining squares #61 and pieced blocks to make 4 corner blocks.

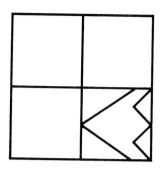

6. Join units in 4 strips of 16 each, turning units to match diagram, forming footprints.

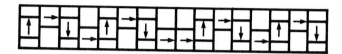

7. Join 2 border strips to opposite sides of quilt center.

8. Stitch 2 corner blocks to each end of remaining border strips. Join to remaining sides of quilt.

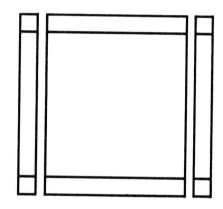

9. Add last frame strips. Miter corners.

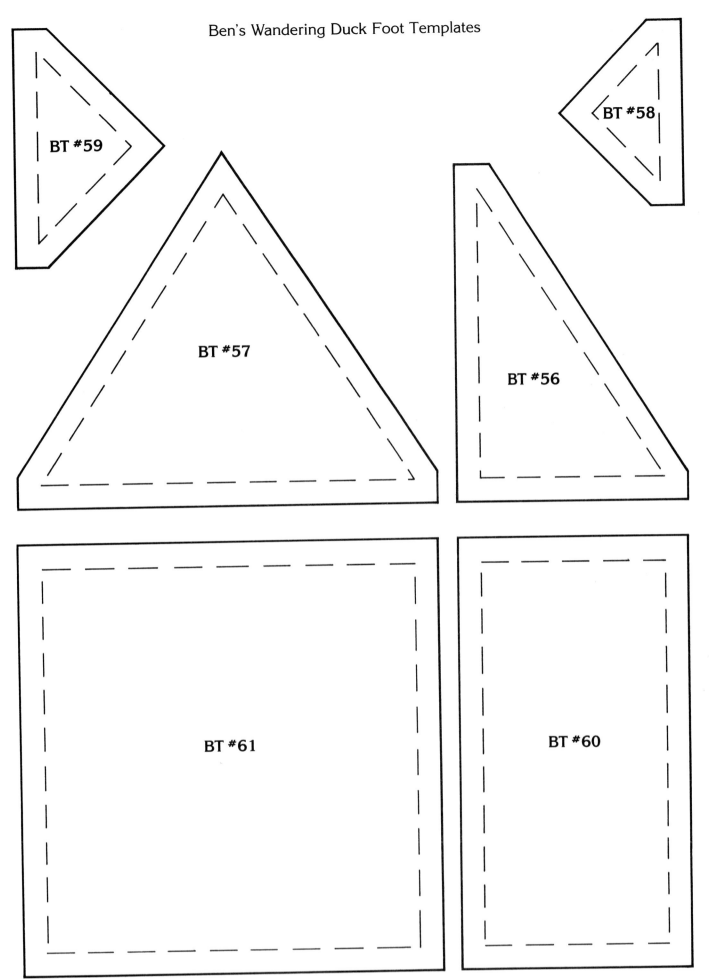

BT #59

BT #58

BT #57

BT #56

BT #61

BT #60

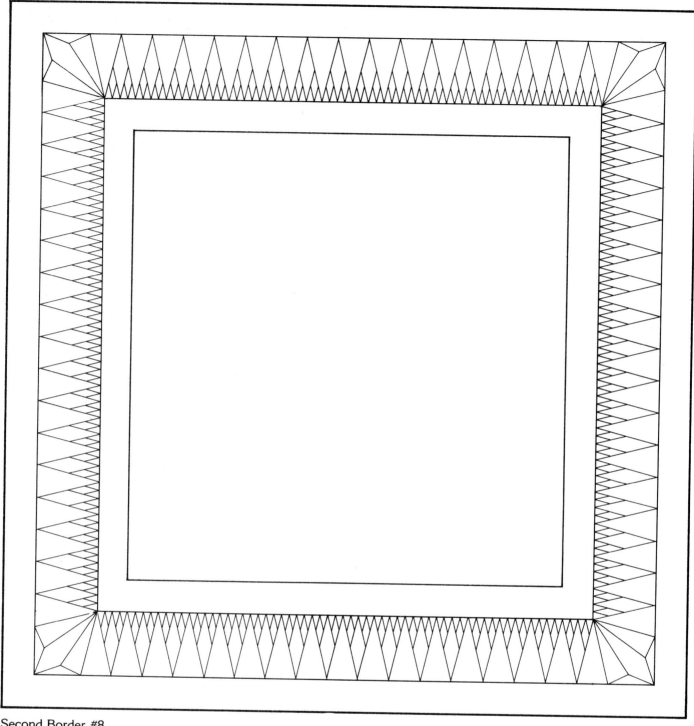

Second Border #8

Shark's Teeth

Anyone who has studied marine life would immediately recognize this adaption of the traditional dog's tooth pattern. The multiple rows of teeth, so characteristic of the shark, would be the perfect final touch to a quilt with a nautical theme. But, don't limit its use because of the name. This is a strong geometric design and it would complement any quilt.

Use BT #62, BT #63, BT #64, BT #65, BT #66, BT #67, and BT #68. The number of pieces you cut from each fabric will depend on the number of colors you use.

PROCEDURE:

1. Join two BT #65 to 2 sides of one BT #64 to form small triangle units.

2. Join two small triangle units to 2 sides of BT #63 to form large triangle units.

3. Add 1 triangle BT #62 to one side of each large triangle unit to make a border unit.

4. Join 16 border units to make each border strip.

5. Construct four corner units following the diagram.

6. Join border strips to all four sides of quilt.

7. Set in corner units.

8. Join frame strips and miter corners.

BT #65

BT #62

BT #63

BT #64

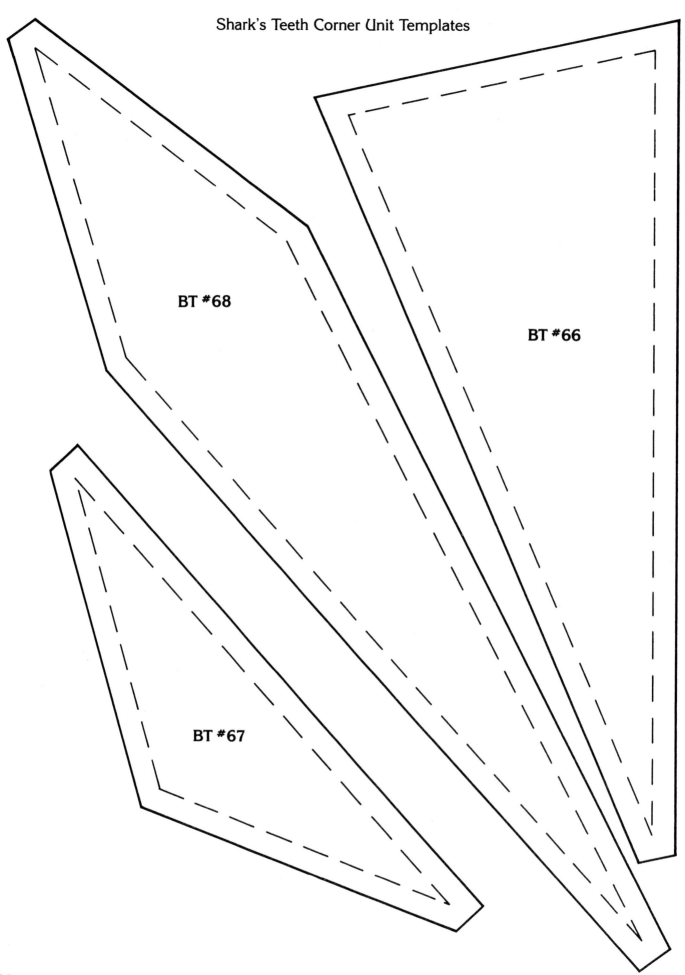

BT #68

BT #66

BT #67

COLOR SELECTION

It wasn't until I had made five or six quilts that I stepped back and realized there was a common quality in all of them. Not in the colors (they were all different colors), but in the tones of the colors and how I had combined them. I had unconsciously expressed my own taste in every one and that is what made them uniquely mine.

Not everyone has made six quilts to go back and study, but we have been making color choices all our lives. I often notice when helping students choose fabrics, that they end up with colors similar to those they are wearing. We all have a color preference and will unconsciously choose that general color range time after time.

I have seen eight people in a class choose red and green fabrics for the same Christmas project and each quilt had a different look when finished. Some people go instantly for the bright reds and greens with Santa Claus and candy cane prints. Others stick to traditional prints with dark (almost turquoise) greens and rich burgundies. Both are equally lovely, yet entirely different and are representative of the maker.

If you are choosing fabrics to coordinate with the color scheme of a particular room, you will probably be as happy with the quilt as you are comfortable in the room. I think it would be a mistake to plan a quilt around the colors of a room you aren't enthusiastic about. The quilt will be new long after the wallpaper and paint have faded away. I have found that quilters who are forced into a particular color scheme often don't finish their work. Remember, not only will you be viewing these colors from across the room, you will view them at close range while you work on them.

Once you have established a color range, it is time to select specific fabrics. Take some time to look at as many quilts or pictures of quilts as you can find. I have heard so many times, "I would never have used those fabrics together and look what a beautiful quilt they make." Look first at the overall quilt. If it is "beautiful" to you, ask yourself why. Study each fabric and how it relates to the others. Colors have an effect on each other. Just as a very dark fabric will make a medium fabric seem lighter, a mauve can be made to look either pink or orange, depending on the fabrics next to it. Be aware that when two or more colors are combined in one calico print, the final effect is a blending of those colors. A blue and yellow print will have a turquoise cast from five feet away. Allow yourself several hours for serious shopping. Remember, there may be safety in following someone else's color plan, but it is not nearly as much fun.

Examine all the fabrics and choose your favorite. It could be light or dark, a small or large print, or a stripe or check. If it is your favorite, use it for the largest portion of the quilt. If it has more than one color, you might want to use that color as an accent.

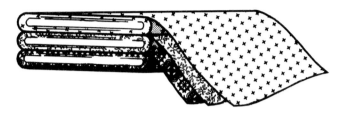

No matter how many colors you choose, it is important to vary the scale. Large and small prints used together give a greater feeling of depth to your quilt. Unfold any bolt of a small print and step away from it. Many small prints form a secondary pattern of stripes or diagonals. That's fine, but you need to be aware of it when you cut large pieces. Stripes and checks move your eye around the quilt and can make the design flow. They can also be used to frame each area of the quilt.

If I use a solid I try to use more than one. But don't feel obliged to use a solid at all. A small print or dot is lovely as a foundation fabric, especially for applique.

Once you have several bolts on the table stand back and squint at them. This limits the amount of light coming into the eye and you will be able to determine if you have a good balance of lights and darks. I like to use at least one bright fabric, but that is why my quilts always look like my quilts.

No matter what colors you choose, you will eventually hear someone say, "I knew that was your quilt. It looks like you." What a compliment! Then you will know you have expressed something of yourself.

FABRIC PLACEMENT

After you have made your fabric choices, the next step is to plan where you will use each fabric in your quilt. Look at the quilts that have one border. These quilts have only two design areas, consequently they must relate very well to each other. My goal in making these smaller quilts was to provide a border that was so well coordinated with the center that the final product gave the effect of a large 64" design rather than a small square with a border added. It isn't necessarily the border shapes that have contributed to this, but the use of the fabrics. Not only are they repeated in the border, but their proportions are repeated also. If the fabrics were used in equal amounts in the center, they are usually repeated in equal amounts in the border.

By the same token, if one color family (or fabric group) was emphasized in the center, it is important to balance it by using larger amounts of the neglected fabrics in the border. Look at the Bouquet of Peonies quilt on page 19. This quilt was made to coordinate with an already existing color scheme. I knew I wanted blue and pink but not mixed in together. A blue center with a pink border seemed the logical solution. Still they needed to be tied together in some way. Bows were the answer. Bringing a small amount of the border color into the center blends them together, making them one. The peony square in the corner was added not only to repeat the design, but also to pull a little bit of blue to the outside edge. That little touch of blue in the border gives the entire design color balance.

When two borders are used there is a lot more leeway for fabric distribution. Look at the Bethlehem Rose Medallion on page 79. Because I had two borders to plan, I could easily divide the fabrics into two groups and use one for each border. You could just as easily use all your fabrics but emphasize different ones in each. Both borders on the Bethlehem Rose Medallion

relate well to the center yet are totally independent of each other. It is the mixing of the colors in the center square that ties all three sections together.

I imagine if you are planning a quilt with two borders you will be using it on a double or queen-size bed. An 88" square is a little large to be hung most places. The second border will be that portion of your quilt that drops off the bed. Keep this in mind when arranging the colors and planning a dust ruffle. I used more blue in the dust ruffle to go with the Bethlehem Rose Medallion quilt because I hadn't used any in the last border.

Don't overlook the importance of the frames as you plan your quilt. The fabric you use to frame each section will determine whether it becomes an integral part of the design or only a buffer between design areas. If you make the frames from the same material used for the background of the center and border, the frame will become part of the background. It separates the two design areas and makes the whole quilt look more spread out. If you have chosen a very "busy" or a solidly colored center and border, they might need the empty area between them. If you use a nonbackground fabric for the frames, as in the Bethlehem Rose Medallion, they become part of the design and must be treated accordingly. Notice that using the striped fabric for diamonds in the center and then repeating it in the border gives the illusion of a square set on the diagonal. The center and borders of both the Bethlehem Rose and Preppie Medallion quilts (see pages 79 and 80) have a lot of background area and can stand being combined with busy frames.

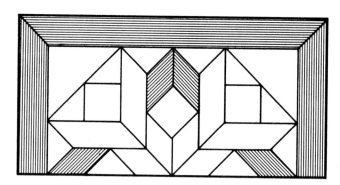

Actually the stripe used in the Preppie Medallion quilt is so bold that it becomes a major element of the quilt design. To have used an equally strong fabric next to it would have diminished them both. I shopped long and hard to find fabrics that would not overpower the stripe, yet would be strong enough to not be overpowered.

I strongly recommend two books for additional reading: *Sampler Supreme* by Catherine H. Anthony and *The Quilter's Album of Block and Borders* by Jinny Beyer. Both books have wonderful information about using stripes.

Of course it is up to you to place the fabrics in your quilt. These observations have been included only as food for thought as you design your own quilt.

ESTIMATING YARDAGE

Most beginning quilters are overwhelmed at the amount of fabric required for a large quilt. So many factors are involved. A lot of the fabric will never make it into the quilt. The cut ends are unusable either from raveling or being cut crooked. The selvages must be cut off. There will be a fabric loss between cut pieces, especially if the fabric has a one-directional print. Even the 1/4" seam allowance takes up more fabric than you would think possible. For this reason alone a quilt with small pieces uses more fabric than one with large pieces.

Use a log cabin quilt as an example. You would think that any strip quilt would be an efficient user of fabric. If your pattern calls for strips 1" wide you must cut them 1 1/2" wide. Therefore, one-third of all the usable material in the quilt is taken up by only the side seams. Even that doesn't take into account the seams at the end of the logs or the wasted short leftovers.

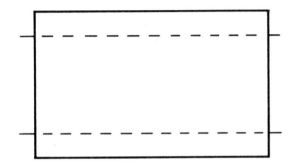

Now that you have designed your quilt, you will have to estimate the yardage requirements yourself. It really isn't as difficult as you think. By following these simple steps, you should be reasonably accurate.

1. Color the final drawing of your quilt.

2. List each fabric and the number of pieces you will be cutting from each one. This is particularly important when estimating for a medallion quilt because you will probably be cutting many different shapes from one piece of material.

3. Using graph paper, lay out a cutting diagram. Make it 42" wide and as long as the paper will allow. Lightly draw in the frame or border strips; then add any smaller pieces you may need from the same material. By taking the time to do this, you will know not only exactly how much material you will need, but you will have had an opportunity to arrange the pieces in the most economical cutting plan.

If you are using a stripe for your frame strips, you will have to count how many times the pattern is repeated across the width of your fabric. Many beautiful patterns are repeated only three times. This results in having to buy twice the length of each frame strip in order to have four complete pattern repeats. This is true even if you are using only 4" of a 12" pattern repeat. The excess fabric in between your chosen stripe can be used for smaller pieces in the body of your quilt, for binding strips, or as an accent.

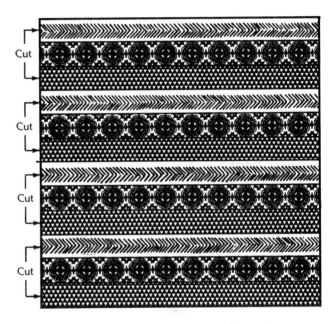

If all of this seems overwhelming, there is a less accurate, more expensive, yet easier method of figuring yardage. I have found that it usually takes about twice as much material to make the top as it does to make the back. If your quilt is double or queen-size, it will usually take 6 yards of material to make the back. You will probably need a total of 12 yards for the front. Guess at what proportion of your quilt top is taken up by the various fabrics. Could it be 50 percent for one and 20 percent and 30 percent for the other two? Then you would need six yards of one fabric, about 2 1/2 yards of another, and about 3 1/2 yards of the third. This is very risky; consequently, when I use this method I usually buy extra for insurance.

If you are duplicating the quilts shown here, you will find the yardage amounts with the pattern for each quilt's center design. This assumes you will be as conservative when you cut your fabric as I am. If you are careful when you cut, you should be fine.

STAR STITCHING HINTS

Although the eight-pointed star is a beautiful pattern, piecing it is sometimes a challenge — stars can have a mind of their own. Following are a few hints that will help you keep them under control:

CUTTING — You will have to mark and cut each piece separately whether you are stitching by hand or by machine. Slip a piece of sandpaper under your fabric before you begin. It will hold your fabric in place as you draw on it.

There are two lines marked on each template in this book. The inner line is the actual finished size. The outer line is the finished size with 1/4" seam allowance added. If you cut your templates on the inner line, you will be drawing the stitching line on the wrong side of your fabric as you trace around them. You must remember to cut 1/4" outside of the line. If, however, you prefer to include the seam allowance in your template, cut the template on the outer line. Then you will be cutting your fabric on the pencil line and stitching 1/4" inside the cut edge.

To conserve fabric, always cut pieces along the longest edge of the material. On a one-yard piece, that is the cut edge; on a two-yard piece, it is the selvage. This makes scraps as long as possible. Should you want to cut border strips for a future project, you might have the necessary length.

GRAIN — When you are cutting pattern pieces from material with a swirly overall pattern or from a solid, paying attention to the fabric grain will make piecing much easier. There are two rules for fabric grain I try to adhere to:

1. Keep the outside of the square on the straight grain of the material.

2. Whenever possible stitch a bias edge to a straight edge. You can accomplish this by marking the diamond template with an arrow along one edge. By keeping this arrow on the straight grain when you cut all of your diamonds, bias and straight will automatically fit together.

If your material has a particular pattern you would like to emphasize, forget all the grain rules and cut any way you want. Stars are perfect for exploring all the different possibilities of fabric pattern designs.

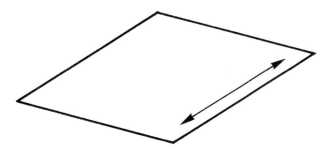

PINNING — When stitching stars, accurate pinning is a must. You must not stitch past the corner point on any piece. The pins will be your guides.

Hold two pieces together and put a pin through each corner point. If you used the template with the seam allowance added, judge by eye 1/4" from each edge and pin there.

Turn the pin and insert to hold the points together. A third pin in the center will hold the seam lines together.

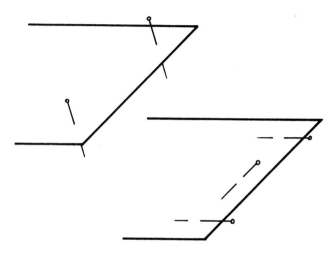

HAND PIECING — Using quilting thread, take a tiny stitch in the corner. Take another stitch in the same place. This is a backstitch and should hold better than a knot. An occasional backstitch along the seam will strengthen it. If you are stitching on a marked line remember to turn and check the back to be certain your stitching marks are still aligned. End by backstitching at the last pin.

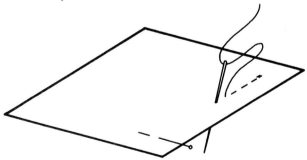

MACHINE PIECING — Machine piecing can be just as accurate as hand piecing if you pin properly. Whether you have marked the stitching line or not, a few additional pins along the seam line will be necessary to keep the pieces under control. Remember you **must not** stitch past the first and last pins. The thread ends must be anchored to prevent the seam from pulling apart. I have good results by adjusting the machine stitch size to "0" and taking two or three stitches in the same place. The machine must be then readjusted to normal stitch size to sew along the seam line; then switch back to "0" to end at the last pin. Backstitching over the first and last few stitches also works well.

RECONSTRUCTING SHAPES — Many of the more complex designs shown here are actually made from very simple traditional patterns. The basic shapes have been divided into smaller pieces which when rejoined form a unit exactly the size of the original shape.

Diamond units are easily constructed by joining the smaller pieces in strips. The strips are then stitched together to form the larger shape.

If you are machine piecing, you will be stitching the seam allowance down. Press the matching seam allowances in opposite directions for a nice flat look.

Whether your diamond points match or not is dependent on the width of the seam allowance. Pay particular attention here. If you have consistently used 1/4" there should not be a problem.

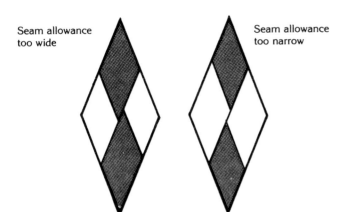

Seam allowance too wide

Seam allowance too narrow

Square units are constructed using the same process. The small squares are joined in strips. The strips are joined to form the large square.

The triangle units are constructed by joining two triangles and one square.

If you have designed a more complex block, follow the same steps. Join smaller shapes in units, then join units to construct a larger shape. The ultimate goal is to always be stitching a straight seam.

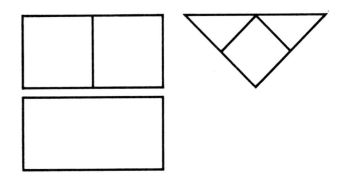

ASSEMBLING STARS — Always join diamonds in pairs, then add the corner squares. You will be fitting in the squares, which is only possible because you have not stitched into the seam allowances. Pin and stitch one side of a square to one diamond, making sure you don't stitch past the pencil line.

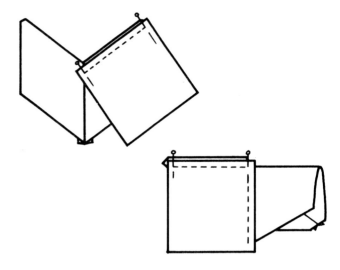

Drop the first diamond and swing square to inside edge of the second diamond. It will fit perfectly. Join two pairs of diamonds to make one-half star. Join half stars in two steps. Pin and stitch from outside to center. Do not go through the middle. Repeat for other side. Add four side triangles.

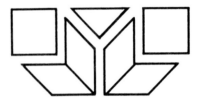

PRESSING — Because you have avoided stitching any seam allowance down, you can hide any irregularities by aggressive pressing. Start in the center of the block. Press all the center seams clockwise. This will evenly distribute the seam allowance and form a little star in the middle. Check the front. Is it perfect? If not, press again in a counterclockwise direction. It should be fine now.

When pressing a seam between two star squares, I go against the rules and press the seam open. I've found if I press to one side, the points of one square roll over and are lost in the seam.

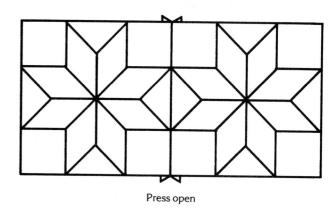

Press open

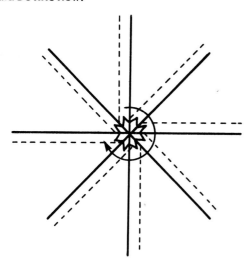

As you move out from the center all of the seams will be pressed in relation to the first ones.

QUILTING STARS — All stars have a tendency to bump up in the middle. If you quilt from the center out (as you should), you will have sixteen knots adding to the bump. You can avoid this by not using a knot at all. Start with a double length of thread. Take one stitch and pull the thread halfway through. Quilt up one side of the diamond with one thread and the other side of the diamond with the other end of the thread. The result — two lines of stitching and no knot.

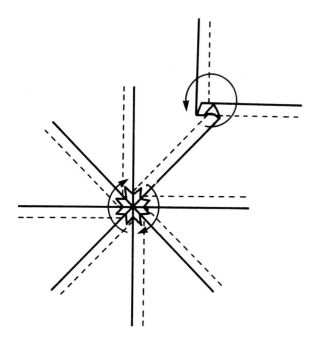

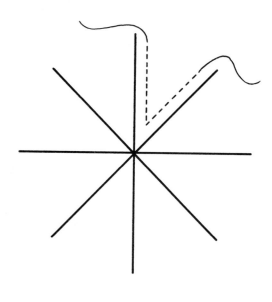

APPLIQUE HINTS

These tips should keep you in control of the applique pieces.

PRESSING TEMPLATES — From file folders or index cards, cut templates the exact finished size of your pattern pieces. Steam press the seam allowance around the stiff edge. Baste the edges under. This is particularly important on the curves of the Dresden Plate.

GATHERING TEMPLATES — Circles and ovals have a tendency to stretch out of shape during the applique process. To maintain control, cut file folder templates the exact finished size of your circle. Run a gathering thread through the seam allowance of the fabric circle. Place cardboard circle on the wrong side of fabric circle and pull the thread to gather the fabric over the cardboard. Press. Applique the circle with gathering template still in it. When finished, clip the back and flip out the cardboard with your fingernail.

STEMS — Curved stems must be cut on the bias. Mark the finished width on the right side of the fabric. Turn and baste edges under. Applique the inside curves first; the outside curves will stretch to fit.

POSITIONING MARKS — A placement diagram has been provided for each applique design included. It is not necessary to transfer the entire pattern to your material. A few strategic points are all you need, such as at the points of the leaves. Don't worry too much if your applique migrates off the positioning marks. Applique is the freest of all quilting techniques. A little variation adds interest.

ANCHORING YOUR THREAD — Because you will use a thread that matches the applique, not the background, there is always the possibility that the thread will migrate out from under the edge of the appliqued piece and show through the background. This can be avoided by taking four or five running stitches through the foundation material under the edge of the applique piece. Then anchor the thread with a backstitch. This secures the thread end at the edge so there is no chance of it being cut when you cut the foundation fabric.

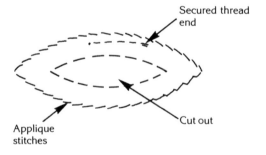

Secured thread end

Cut out

Applique stitches

THE STITCH — Applique wears on the edge first, consequently your quilt will wear longer and look nicer if your edges are firmly secured.

After anchoring the thread, bring the needle straight up from the back through the foundation fabric, catching a few threads of the applique piece. Push the needle down through the foundation fabric only, very close to the point where the needle came up. If you move too far away from this point your applique will look like a hem.

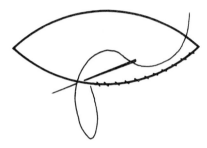

I cannot overemphasize the importance of using an applique needle. It is a very fine, flexible needle. It will make a big difference in your work.

CUTTING THE FOUNDATION FABRIC — This very easy step will make a big difference in the finished square. Separate the applique from the foundation fabric, then snip the foundation fabric just enough to slide the scissors inside. Trim 1/4" from the edge using the stitches as a guide. Doing this will not only make the applique lie flatter, but will eliminate the possibility of having to quilt through extra layers of material. Your stitches will be more uniform and your fingers will thank you.

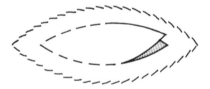

PRESSING — Press from the back into a terry towel. This will give the design more relief. If you must press the front, do not slide the iron. That will result in the "shinys."

ADDING FRAMES AND MITERING

All frame strips are cut 4 1/2" wide. Determine the length of the frame strips by taking the size of the square plus two times the width of the frame strips.

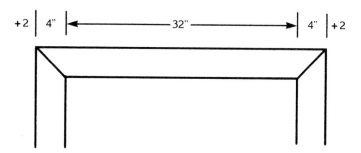

Add another 4" for insurance. In this case it would be 32 + 4 + 4 + 4 = 44. The frame strip for the center square is cut 44" x 4 1/2". The frame around the first border is cut 68" x 4 1/2". The frame around the second border is cut 92" x 4 1/2".

Fold the strip in half to find the center and mark it with a pin. Using the middle pin as a guide, measure and mark the strip the exact finished size of the piece to be framed. The mark should be 1/4" from the cut edge.

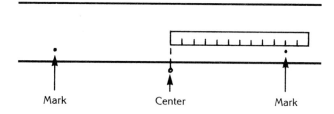

Use your Multi-Miter™ to mark the exact seam line of the mitered corner by placing the angle marked with a square at the premeasured end point. Align horizontal marking with cut edge to make sure it is straight. Draw miter seam along angled edge of the Multi-Miter™.

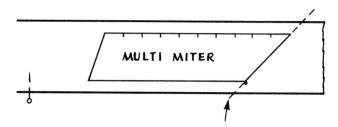

Flip Multi-Miter™ and mark other end of frame strip. Pin strip to quilt and stitch, being careful not to stitch past the end pins. The stitching lines should meet, not overlap.

Fold quilt on diagonal to match the miter seams. Pin and stitch miter. Trim and press seam to one side.

The same process is used to miter the borders on an octagonal quilt. Use the angle of the Multi-Miter™ that is marked with an octagon. If a Multi-Miter™ is not available in your area, you can still miter the corner of an octagon by eye.

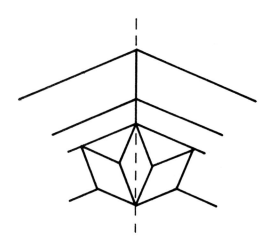

Fold the frame strips back until they have formed a seam that is in a straight line with the quilt center. Because all of these patterns use forty-five degree diamonds, the chances are very good that your pattern will point out the correct angle for you.

The following measurements are the lengths of the sides of the octagons:

32" octagon - side is 13.25"
16" octagon - side is 6.62"
12" octagon - side is 4.96"
 8" octagon - side is 3.31"
 6" octagon - side is 2.48"
 4" octagon - side is 1.65"
 3" octagon - side is 1.24"

Whether you are using a Multi-Miter™ or are using traditional mitering methods, it's very important to take the time to measure and mark each border strip. The edge of a pieced block has a lot of "give." When stitching an unpieced strip to a pieced quilt, one stretches and the other doesn't. Your frame can look almost ruffled.

BINDING YOUR QUILT

Cut your binding strips 1 1/2" wide and 4" longer than the side of your quilt. Fold matching long edges and press. Open and fold raw edges to center crease and press again.

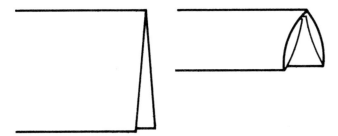

Open binding strips and pin right sides together, matching raw edges of quilt top. Leave 2" extra binding at each end. Stitch from end pin to end pin in first crease through all layers. Repeat on remaining three sides. Now trim excess batting and backing from quilt edge. Waiting until this point to trim the backing and batting assures that your batting is secured to the edge of the quilt and the binding will not be "empty."

1. Working from the back of the quilt, use Multi-Miter™ to mark the miter seam lines on the binding strips. Miter each corner.

2. Trim corner from binding (following diagram) across the outside crease.

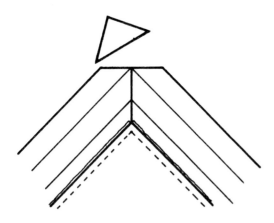

3. Fold clipped corner in at second crease.

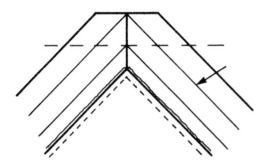

4. Fold straight edges of binding along outside crease.

5. Make second fold along center crease. The two edges should form a perfect miter. Blind stitch binding on back.

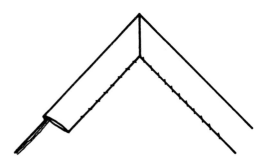

Mitering the binding on an octagon is slightly different.

1. Stitch eight binding strips to top of octagon and miter seams. DO NOT CLIP CORNER.

2. Fold corner over twice. This is a little bulky.

3. Blind stitch one piece of binding up to point of miter.

4. Trim excess fabric. Fold second piece of fabric over to appear to be mitered. Blind stitch in place. Continue blind stitching around the quilt and make the "mock miter" at each seam.

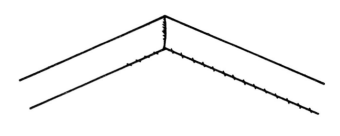

BIBLIOGRAPHY

Anthony, Catherine H., *Sampler Supreme,* Santa Clara, California: Leone Publishing Company, 1983.

Beyer, Jinny, *The Quilters Album of Blocks and Borders,* McLean, Virginia: EPM Publications, Inc., 1980.

Thompson, Shirley, *The Finishing Touch,* Edmonds, Washington: Powell Publications, 1980.

Thompson, Shirley, *It's Not a Quilt Until It's Quilted,* Edmonds, Washington: Powell Publications, 1984.

That Patchwork Place Publications

B54	**Barnyard Beauties** by Mary Ann Farmer	4.00
B56	**Fabriscapes™** by Gail Johnson	5.00
B57	**Be An Angel** by Mary Ann Farmer	4.00
B58	**Special Santas** by Mary Ann Farmer	4.00
B62	**The Basics of Quilted Clothing** by Nancy Martin	8.00
B65	**Small Quilts** by Marsha McCloskey	6.00
B66	**Pilots, Partners & Pals** by Mary Ann Farmer	4.00
B68	**Warmest Witches to You** by Mary Ann Farmer	4.00
B70	**Country Christmas** by Sue Saltkill	6.00
B71	**Wall Quilts** by Marsha McCloskey	8.00
B72	**Cathedral Window - A New View** by Mary Ryder Kline	6.00
B74	**The Stencil Patch** by Nancy J. Martin	6.00
B75	**Sew Special** by Susan A. Grosskopf	6.00
B76	**A Quilter's Christmas** by Nancyann Twelker	8.00
B77	**Housing Projects** by Nancy J. Martin	9.95
B78	**Projects for Blocks and Borders** by Marsha McCloskey	11.95
B79	**Linens and Old Lace** by Nancy Martin and Sue Saltkill	9.95
B80	**A Touch of Fragrance** by Marine Bumbalough	5.95
B81	**Bearwear** by Nancy J. Martin	7.95
B82	**Christmas Classics** by Sue Saltkill	6.95
B83	**Christmas Quilts** by Marsha McCloskey	11.95
B85	**Branching Out: Tree Quilts** by Carolann Palmer	11.95
B86	**Template - Free Quiltmaking** by Trudie Hughes	11.95
B87	**Pieces of the Past** by Nancy J. Martin	16.95

ABOUT THE AUTHOR

Kathy is a gifted designer with an instinctive eye for color. Her degree in design from the University of Maryland, and its accompanying drafting courses, has laid the foundation for a varied career during which she has traveled extensively throughout the eastern United States, teaching and giving workshops.

Inspired by her grandmother's stitchery, Kathy has focused her considerable artistic talent on needlecrafts. She made her first colorful and intricately designed quilts for use in her own home. After winning numerous awards, she began teaching her techniques to others. The demand for her services as a teacher and lecturer has continued to grow, because Kathy does more than just provide instructions on how to reproduce her designs. Her teaching and writing inspire self-confidence and encourage creativity. She offers her students and her readers the key to their own storehouse of quilted treasures.

Printed in United States of America